The Anointed One Of Many Colors

ELLA CURRIE-JOHNSON

Anionted One Of Many Colors

Copyright © 2021 Ella Currie-Johnson
All rights reserved.
ISBN:9798811478019

No part of this publication may be reproduced, stored in or introduced into a retrieval system, or transmitted, in any form or by any means, electronic, mechanical, photocopying, recording or otherwise without prior permission from the copyright owner.

Unless otherwise indicated, all scripture quotations are taken from The Holy Bible, King James Version

Scriptures marked NKJV are taken from the NEW KING JAMES VERSION (NKJV): Scripture taken from the NEW KING JAMES VERSION®. Copyright© 1982 by Thomas Nelson, Inc. Used by permission. All rights reserved.

Please note the writing style in this book chooses to capitalize certain pronouns in Scripture that refer to God the Father, the Son, and the Holy Spirit, and may differ from other publishing styles.

Cover/Interior design by Clarissa Currie Wilson

DEDICATION

Affectionately dedicated to my deceased father and mother, Blount Currie and Clydia Mae Baggett Currie, whose seeds shaped my life.

CONTENTS

	Introduction	i
1	New Life	1
2	See The Holy Ghost Move	7
3	Harvest Upon Harvest	16
4	Colorful Walk With God	26
5	Tragedy Came	34
6	Receive God's Love and Give It Away	42
7	House of Prayer	52
8	Desiring the Holy Ghost	60
9	Powerful Testimonies	74
10	Prayers	93
	Epilogue	99
	Pictures	101
	About The Author	109

ACKNOWLEDGMENTS

First and foremost, to God our Father, to the Son, Jesus, and Holy Spirit who led me to write this book.

I wish to express my deepest appreciation to my children, Dexter, Clarissa, and Vendia, for their constant support and encouragement.

Many thanks to Lydia Maxine Moore for keeping me accountable for completing this book.

Special thanks to friends and family who gratefully shared powerful testimonies that testify of the goodness of God.

Clarissa Currie Wilson, you are truly a gift. Thank you for your diligence, focus, editing, and your late-night dedication to see this book come to fruition. What a joy and delight to work on this book with you. Thanks so much for sharing your creativity and insight.

Tomeka Robinson, Thank you for your keen eyes and editing skills.

But with the precious blood of Christ, as of a lamb without blemish and without spot. He indeed was foreordained before the foundation of the world but was manifest in these last times for you who through Him believe in God, who raised Him from the dead and gave Him glory, so that your faith and hope are in God. 1 Peter 1:19-21 **NKJV**

INTRODUCTION

There is a rainbow in the clouds. This book is an exploration of promises and the goodness of God. God keeps ALL His promises but somehow in today's world many have lost sight of the promises of God.
    During the life of my mother I saw an abundance of His promises miraculously manifest. However, today I ponder where are all the miracles, signs, and wonders? Jesus Christ is the same yesterday, today and forever. Could it be that we are not crying out to the Mighty One who puts rainbows in the clouds as a symbol of His promises? Are we losing hope when we see so many depressed, diseased, and oppressed, people in the world? Have we forgotten that the earth is the Lords and everything in it belongs to Him? Have we forgotten what happens when the Spirit of the Lord rests upon a person as written in Luke chapter 4 verse 18? There is a stirring in my spirit that seeks a revival like never before.
    As you journey through the life of my mom. You will find an exploration of faith, courage and enlightment of the promises of God. While you ponder the ways of God I hope you too would cry out for revival.
    Growing up we were Christians and believed in the power of God. As I have grown to know the power of God I often connect it to the greater works Jesus mentioned in scripture. Jesus said, "Most assuredly, I say to you, he who believes in Me, the works that I do he will do also; and greater works than these he will do, because I go to My Father. And whatever you ask in My name, that I will do, that the Father may be glorified in the Son. If you ask anything in My name, I will do it."
    We still live in an era of greater works. I believe there are so many greater works to manifest in the name of Jesus. When we really sit and ponder the blessings of God we noticed that they always flow from God through a person

to others. With that being said, God sends a rainbow full of His promised blessings which manifest His greater works through a yielded vessel to another vessel. He wants to pour out His rich oil that sets the captives free. The bible does say where the Spirit of the Lord is there is liberty.

It's time for a refreshing in the Holy Ghost and a hunger for deeper revelation of the word of God. It's time for the vessels of God to wake up and rise to what God has called them to be. It's time for the rainbows to show up and illuminate the power of God. Let us all step up and move in God's timing.

CHAPTER 1

NEW LIFE

On December 3, 1927, a baby was born to late Troy and Mae Baggett. They lived on a farm in Godwin, North Carolina, a small town in Sampson County. This little baby was their third child, and little did they know that God had a great plan for her, that someday she would be called "Anointed One Of Many Colors."

As I begin to tell the true mission of the one known as *"Anointed One Of Many Colors,"* I pray God would enlarge your faith and bless you that you too would desire to be the one He called you to be. God has great plans for each one of us, and may your plans always align with His plans.

For I know the thoughts that I think toward you, saith the Lord, thoughts of peace, and not of evil, to give you an expected end. Jeremiah 29:11

When I was a child, I did things as a child. Now that I have grown mature spiritually and understand God's ways. It's such an honor and blessing to be able to share the life of the one I call *"Anointed One Of Many Colors,"* my mother, Clydia Baggett Currie. She fulfilled the shoes of one of my favorite scriptures, Proverbs 31. She was surely blessed and highly favored by God. God could trust that she would live holy and righteous before Him.

When I was a child, I spoke as a child, I understood as a child, I thought as a child; but when I became a man, I put away childish things.
1 Corinthians 13:11

Who can find a virtuous wife? For her worth is far above rubies. The heart of her husband safely trusts her; So he will have no lack of gain. She does him good and not evil. All the days of her life. She seeks wool and flax, And willingly works with her hands. She is like the merchant ships, She brings her food from afar. She also rises while it is yet night, and provides food for her household, And a portion for her maidservants. She considers a field and buys it; From her profits she plants a vineyard. She girds herself with strength, And strengthens her arms. She perceives that her merchandise is good, And her lamp does not go out by night. She stretches out her hands to the distaff, And her hand holds the spindle. She extends her hand to the poor, Yes, she reaches out her hands to the needy. She is not afraid of snow for her household, for all her household is clothed with scarlet. She makes tapestry for herself; Her clothing is fine linen and purple. Her husband is known in the gates, When he sits among the elders of the land. She makes linen garments and sells them, And supplies sashes for the merchants. Strength and honor are her clothing; She shall rejoice in time to come. She opens her mouth with wisdom, And on her tongue is the law of kindness. She watches over the ways of her household, And does not eat the bread of idleness. Her children rise up and call her blessed; Her husband also, and he praises her: "Many daughters have done well, But you excel them all" Charm is deceitful and beauty is passing, But a woman who fears the Lord, she shall be praised. Give her of the fruit of her hands, And let her own works praise her in the gates. Proverbs 31:10-31 NKJV

Even in times of trouble, her faith in God would never waiver. Mom was a true woman of faith and a fierce prayer warrior much like David. Mom lived a life led by the Holy Spirit. Never would she hurt anyone or try to fight anyone that would hurt her. She always kept a posture of meekness and humility. There were so many lessons to learn from her. Throughout her life, she had to shed many tears, but through the pain, she always knew God was more powerful than pain. She trusted and believed that God was a healer of ALL infirmities. Mom consistently prayed for God to increase her strength. She taught me that we do not do anything in our own strength but through the strength of God.

She knew God's ways were perfect, and I totally agree. Jesus is the very image of how we should handle everything. Mom instilled in her children to always live our lives God's way; by the word of God.

Now also when I am old and gray headed, O God, do not forsake me, Until I declare Your strength to this generation, Your power to everyone who is to come. Also Your righteousness, O God, is very high, You who have done great things; O God, who is like You? Psalm 71:18-19 NKJV

Fear thou not; for I am with thee: be not dismayed; for I am thy God: I will strengthen thee; yea, I will help thee; yea, I will uphold thee with the right hand of my righteousness. Isaiah 41:10

> *In the day when I cried thou answeredst me, and strengthenedst me with strength in my soul.* Psalm 138:3

> *I can do all things through Christ which strengtheneth me.* Philippians 4:13

> *He gives power to the weak, And to those who have no might He increases strength.* Isaiah 40:29 NKJV

> *Trust in the Lord with all thine heart; and lean not unto thine own understanding. In all thy ways acknowledge him, and he shall direct thy paths.* Proverbs 3:5-6

> *For whom He foreknew, He also predestined to be conformed to the image of His Son, that He might be the first born among brethren.* Romans 8:29 NKJV

My mission is to continue to seek God, trust Him, live by His word, and spread the gospel as I was taught. It has been such a pleasurable life to be brought up in an environment of a God-fearing mother. Mom loved Jesus and taught me to love Jesus with all my heart. That is truly the best gift one can give. Sharing Jesus with your family and the world has great rewards!

> *And he answering said, "Thou shalt love the Lord thy God with all thy heart, and with all thy soul, and with all thy strength, and with all thy mind, and thy neighbor as thyself."* Matthew 22:37-39 NKJV

But without faith it is impossible to please Him, for he who comes to God must believe that He is, and that He is a rewarder of those who diligently seek Him. Hebrews 11:6 NKJV

† Prayer

Heavenly Father, my creator, and my glory, I lift Your name above all things, and I give You praise and honor for being such a good and faithful Father. I am so grateful for Jesus and the Holy Spirit that led me to write this book. I lift this book up to You with gratitude for giving me a precious gem that forever shines bright in my heart. I thank You for allowing her to be a vessel for Your kingdom. As I have written this book unto You, I pray that it will be an enlightening inspiration to all readers. May they sense Your presence and grow to know You on a deeper level. I pray that they will forever be blessed beyond measure in the name of Jesus.

CHAPTER 2

SEE THE HOLY GHOST MOVE

It was around the late 50s early 60s when the Holy Ghost took place in the life of my mother. During the spring, a traveling minister held a tent revival in our community. It was a huge tent that was placed on the ground over a large area of golden-brown sawdust. Perhaps the sawdust was used as a floor cushion. Crowds would show up each night, and there was lots of singing, praising, and tambourine beating worshipers. The minister was a beautiful powerful woman of God. She was bold as a lion, very confident, and spoke with great authority. She preached powerful sermons. God flowed through her miraculously. It was beyond amazement in my little eyes to see such a powerful woman minister. After each sermon, she would always ask if anyone needed healing, salvation, or wanted to be filled with the Holy Ghost.

One night during the revival services, the minister asked, "Is there anyone who wants to be filled with the Holy Ghost?" I looked around because I didn't have a clue as to what she was talking about. People started walking up front and formed a prayer line. The minister prayed for everyone individually who got in line. Mom got in the line too. When she started praying for mom, she began to speak in an unknown tongue, just as it is written on the Day of Pentecost in the book of Acts. Mom had received a heavenly language that was unknown to our entire family.

Not knowing what was happening, the minister said to her, "it's the Holy Ghost, and I will teach you all about it." This is where it all began for my mom. God's purpose for her ministry began that night. The Holy Ghost made a major difference in her life and in the lives of many people; ones who knew her and ones who didn't know her at all. God is no respecter of person as He shows no partiality. He loves us all with an everlasting heart, and His desire is that we all come into truth to be saved and receive the Holy Ghost.

And when the day of Pentecost was fully come, they were all with one accord in one place. And suddenly there came a sound from heaven as of a rushing mighty wind, and it filled all the house where they were sitting. And there appeared unto them cloven tongues like as of fire, and it sat upon each of them. And they were all filled with the Holy Ghost, and began to speak with other tongues, as the Spirit gave them utterance.
Acts 2:1-4

Then Peter opened his mouth, and said, of a truth I perceive that God is no respecter of persons: But in every nation he that feareth him, and worketh righteousness, is accepted with him.
Acts 10:34-35

The Lord hath appeared of old unto me, saying, Yea, I have loved thee with an everlasting love: therefore with lovingkindness have I drawn thee.
Jeremiah 31:3

However, when He, the Spirit of truth, has come, He will guide you into all truth; for He will not speak on His own authority, but whatever He hears He will speak; and He will tell you things to come. John 16:13

For this is good and acceptable in the sight of God our Savior, who desires all men to be

saved and to come to the knowledge of the truth.
1 Timothy 2:3-4 NKJV

I would that ye all spake with tongues but rather that ye prophesied: for greater is he that prophesieth than he that speaketh with tongues, except he interpret, that the church may receive edifying. 1 Corinthians 14:5

Faithfully the minister kept her word and started coming to our house to teach mom all about what was going on inside her spirit. She was an outstanding teacher, full of love, tender and compassionate. She took time to pray, read the bible, and thoroughly explain the Holy Ghost to mom while I would sit and listen. The bible speaks about God giving us shepherds after His heart, who will feed us with knowledge and understanding. She carried a genuine shepherding heart. She reminded me of the biblical apostles that taught in the New Testament. She taught with such anticipation. She explained that the Holy Ghost was the helper Jesus spoke about in the book of John. I can truly say the helper showed up and took resident in my mom. Mom only had a first-grade education, and all the spiritual knowledge that flowed out of her came directly from the Spirit of God.

But the Comforter, which is the Holy Ghost, whom the Father will send in my name, he shall teach you all things, and bring all things to your remembrance, whatsoever I have said unto you.
John 14:26

As mom continued to spend time with the Lord, she spent lots of time speaking in unknown tongues, lamenting, and praying. She would pray for hours at times. Mom would pray for daddy, her children, sisters, brothers, all family members, friends, and all prayer requests. Often people would call her on the phone and request prayer as well. Our phone was basically a prayer line in as much as a prayer line in the church.

God graced her with the gift of healing, laying on of hands, and the gift of faith. Often the Spirit of the Lord would rest on mom, revealing His Spirit of wisdom and understanding, counsel, might, and knowledge as she would pray for individuals. She prayed for all people, all races, no matter what side of the tracks you were from, who you were or whatever your condition was. I remember just before she would pray for people, she would always ask them, "do you believe that the Lord will heal you?" "Now you got to have faith in God, not me. It's God that heals you. You give Him the glory and praise." She would always give God all the glory. God is so glorious, and He deserves all the honor, praise, and glory. People would stop by our house both day and night for prayer. Mom would always make room to pray for them. There were many times when the Spirit of knowledge would fall upon her, and she could immediately sense where they were hurting and feel their pain. Mom would lay hands on the area and pray thereafter; the pain would cease. There were so many miracles that took place right in front of my eyes.

> *And these signs shall follow them that believe; In my name shall they cast out devils; they shall speak with new tongues; They shall take up serpents; and if they drink any deadly thing, it shall not hurt them; they shall lay hands on the sick, and they shall recover.* Mark 16:17-18

> *Now when the sun was setting, all they that had any sick with divers diseases brought them unto him; and he laid his hands on every one of them, and healed them.* Luke 4:40

There are diversities of gifts, but the same Spirit. There are differences of ministries, but the same Lord. And there are diversities of activities, but it is the same God who works all in all. But the manifestation of the Spirit is given to each one for the profit of all: for to one is given the word of wisdom through the Spirit, to another the word of knowledge through the same Spirit, to another faith by the same Spirit, to another gifts of healing the same Spirit, to another the working of miracles, to another prophecy, to another discerning of spirits, to another different kinds of tongues, to another the interpretation of tongues. But one and the same Spirit works all these things, distributing to each one individually as He wills. 1 Corinthians 12:4-11 NKJV

And Jesus said unto them, Because of your unbelief: for verily I say unto you, If ye have faith as a grain of mustard seed, ye shall say unto this mountain, Remove hence to yonder place; and it shall remove; and nothing shall be impossible unto you. Matthew 17:20

One of my most prominent memories from moms praying moments was when a visitor came by with a stomach tumor. Mom prayed for her, and the tumor dissolved. The visitor was overjoyed because when she went back to the doctor, he told her that it wasn't there anymore. To God be the Glory! God has revealed His miraculous healing power so many times before my eyes that I can't stop telling the goodness of the Lord. No matter the situation or circumstance, God is good all the time.

Is any among you afflicted? let him pray. Is any merry? let him sing psalms. Is any sick among you? let him call for the elders of the church; and let them pray over him, anointing him with oil in the name of the Lord: And the prayer of faith shall save the sick, and the Lord shall raise him up; and if he have committed sins, they shall be forgiven him. Confess your faults one to another, and pray one for another, that ye may be healed. The effectual fervent prayer of a righteous man availeth much. James 5:13-16

O give thanks unto the Lord, for he is good: for his mercy endureth forever Psalm 107:1

Mom was an outstanding wife and mother. She had one boy and five girls. We were very young when the Holy Ghost started to move in our mother's life. I was about six years old. It was something new to all of us. My siblings and I had noticed a major change in mom and really didn't understand it, but we knew it was something good for all of us. We had not seen the Holy Ghost move in church before. The Holy Ghost fell upon the church we were attending during the late fifties, and it was a move that no one had ever experienced before. All we could do was cry. It wasn't a fearful cry; it was more like joyful tears.

I recall during those days that the church was very quiet, and there were little to no responses to the sermons. There was no praising God out loud or glorifying God freely; however, when mom received the Holy Ghost, things started changing. There was a major change in how she responded in church. As she welcomed the Holy Ghost and grew in the knowledge of God, she wanted everyone to encounter the Holy Ghost. She was very vocal that Jesus had forgiven her sins, and she had accepted Him as her Lord and Savior. She expressly let it be known that there would be no more sitting down on God. She let the Holy Ghost move as the utterances came. She would praise the Lord and sometimes even shout and dance before the Lord. It was such a pleasure seeing mom glow in the presence of the Lord. She lived a spirit-filled life. Mom was a mighty woman of God, full of wisdom and understanding. She was a powerful prayer warrior. Mom constantly prayed for the sick, soul salvations, and Holy Ghost recipients.

> *And these signs shall follow them that believe; In my name shall they cast out devils; they shall speak with new tongues; They shall take up serpents; and if they drink any deadly thing, it shall not hurt them; they shall lay hands on the sick, and they shall recover.* Mark 16:17-18

> *That if thou shalt confess with thy mouth the Lord Jesus, and shalt believe in thine heart that God hath raised him from the dead, thou shalt be saved. For with the heart man believeth unto righteousness; and with the mouth confession is made unto salvation.* Romans 10:9-10

> *But ye shall receive power, after that the Holy Ghost is come upon you: and ye shall be witnesses unto me both in Jerusalem, and in all Judaea, and in Samaria, and unto the uttermost part of the earth.* Acts 1:8

Let us pause for a minute and give God the highest praise. HALLELUJAH! He is worthy of all praise and honor. Thank you, Lord!

> *Enter into his gates with thanksgiving, and into his courts with praise: be thankful unto him, and bless his name.* Psalm 100:4

† Prayer

Heavenly Father, I give You praise and honor for being such a good and faithful father. I am beyond grateful for allowing me to experience the great move of the Holy Ghost in my mom back in the mid-1900s. I thank You for the shepherding minister who mentored my mom with great knowledge and understanding of You as written in Jeremiah 3:15. I thank You for everyone that was healed, every soul that was saved, and everyone who received Your gift of the Holy Ghost. Today I lift everyone who has chosen to read this book. I pray that they, too, will desire to move to a higher level of Your spirit. I pray that You, the Mighty One, would fill everyone who desires to be filled with the Holy Ghost. I pray that You will save every lost soul and increase their hunger for more of You. May You increase Your anointing on all who have already received but have stagnated. In Jesus' Name!

CHAPTER 3

HARVEST UPON HARVEST

Not only was mom graced spiritually, but she was also graced with many other talents. She always worked hard as laborer for the Lord. She was also a seamstress and an outstanding cook. She and daddy were both highly skilled farmers and prosperous sharecroppers. We had tobacco, cotton, farm animals, and large vegetable gardens.

Along with her ministry, mom was a seamstress at heart. She made most of our clothes during our early years. Mom also made quilts, bonnets, and aprons from the leftover cloth. She knew how to repurpose almost anything.

As part of mom's continuous fellowship with saints, she would have huge Sunday meals after church. I called it soul food Sunday. Southern cooked food that was just good for your soul, and of course, the Spirit of the Lord was always there. Mom would invite the pastor's family and others from the church to join us for soul food Sunday. She was known for being a great cook. She loved to cook chicken pastry, collard greens, cornbread, fried chicken, and potato salad.

As sharecroppers, our entire family would work the land all summer long without payment. Settlement payments for sharing crops of tobacco and cotton were normally released in the month of November. The net income was a smidgen of what it should have been; however, mom and dad always managed finances well. Most of the income was used to pay summer debts, Christmas shopping, managing basic household bills and supplies for the winter.

At the home front, we had chickens, pigs, and lots of plant-based foods. We always had plenty of meat, fruits, and vegetables to eat and lots to share. Without a price, mom enjoyed sharing food with others. Mom was a giver and lived on the scripture; "it's better to give than receive."

> *I have shown you in every way, by laboring like this, that you must support the weak. And remember the words of the Lord Jesus, that He said, 'It is more blessed to give than to receive.'* " Acts 20:35 NKJV

> *Give, and it will be given to you: good measure, pressed down, shaken together, and running over will be put into your bosom. For with the same measure that you use, it will be measured back to you.*" Luke 6:38 NKJV

As a child growing up on a farm, we basically had a family produce/meat market for our household and others. I guess that would make mom and dad butchers. They knew how to process meat as if they were USDA certifiers. What a great accomplishment for being self-taught. Mom also knew how to preserve both fruits and vegetables so that we never had to purchase those items in the grocery store. She would always can tomatoes, and make pear, grape, and peach jam. Mom also loved blanching and freezing all kinds of vegetables to ensure that we had plenty of food for the winter. Our annually garden was always filled with tomatoes, collards, cabbage, cucumbers, field peas, butterbeans, corn, watermelons and so much more.

The Fall season was one of my favorite times of the year because I love how our family would gather to process meat for the winter season. It was more like a celebration. Our family, inclusive of several extended family members, would gather in the front yard to harvest hogs. They all worked well together as a production team. Each one used their individual skills to successfully prepare a substantial amount of meat for the winter.

Dad would start preparing a day before the harvest. He would dig an enormous hole and place wood logs in it so that they could heat water to a scalding temperature for cleaning the hog. The hole had to be big enough to hold a big drum that looked like a bathtub. The drum is where they would place the hog in order to remove the hair. They would fill the drum full of water thereafter; when the temperature reached a scalding point, the hog would be lowered, fully submerged, and rolled around several times. The process would soften the hair follicles to make it easy to scrape off the hair. Next, they would scape off all the hair.

Once the hog was fully hair-free, they would lift the hog out of the water using a homemade hoist connected to a tractor lift. Then they would hose down the hog to get it cleaned thoroughly. Subsequently, my uncle would cut the hog open and remove all the insides, including the intestines. My mother and aunt would be ready to clean the intestines because they use them for casing sausage and liver pudding. I even got to pour water into the intestines to help with the cleaning process. Simultaneously, dad and my uncles would be salting all the other meat parts, such as ham, pork chops, bacon, and tenderloin, for persevering. Afterwards, all the meat was hung in the smokehouse for the winter.

It was such a wonderful time being a part of our family's unique manufacturing production system for meat preserving. From the rising of the sun to the going down of the sun, everybody truly enjoyed great fellowship, conversations, and lots of laughter. We even got to partake in a buffet full of fresh meat and vegetables. It was lots of fun and a lot of hard work, but it was well worth all our efforts. Most of the time, we finished up all the loose ends the next day. Those were two of the best family days ever.

Another one of our manufacturing products was chickens. Chickens were one of mom's favorite farm animals. She loved caring for her chickens. There were times she even brought the baby chickens inside so they would stay warm from the cold winter nights. The harvesting of chickens was such a delight because mom could cook the best chicken pastry in the area. There was always an abundance of eggs too. So much so that mom sold fresh eggs by the dozen.

Although mom was a self-taught businesswoman at heart, she also was a giver. I can remember many weekends when visitors would stop by and before they would leave their hands would be full. Mom would take bags out to the smokehouse and filled them full of meat; ham, sausage, and liver pudding, along with food she had canned for the winter.

Oh, what marvelous reminiscences remain in my heart because the 1969 Smokehouse that was built by daddy and one of our neighbors is still standing today. It is such a great memorial that I call it Jehovah Jireh because God truly provided back then, and He continues to keep all His promises today. Mom was known to have faith like Abraham, and when God provided a ram in the thicket, Abraham, too, called the place Jehovah Jireh.

And Abraham lifted up his eyes, and looked, and behold behind him a ram caught in a thicket by his horns: and Abraham went and took the ram and offered him up for a burnt offering in the stead of his son. And Abraham called the name of that place Jehovah Jireh: as it is said to this day, In the mount of the Lord it shall be seen. Genesis 22:13-14

"Therefore, do not worry, saying, 'What shall we eat?' or 'What shall we drink?' or 'What shall we wear?' For after all these things the Gentiles seek. For your heavenly Father knows that you need all these things. But seek first the kingdom of God and His righteousness, and all

these things shall be added to you. Therefore do not worry about tomorrow, for tomorrow will worry about its own things. Sufficient for the day is its own trouble. Matthew 6:31-34 NKJV

There were so many times I saw mom giving away food. I remember saying to her if you give our food away, we will not have anything to eat. She looked at me with a big smile and replied, "have you ever gone to bed hungry?" I said, "no." I'm quite sure mom was pondering on the promises of God when she answered my question as it is written in chapter thirty-seven in the book of Psalms. That was a good lesson for me because she taught me many of the ways of God not only through the life she lived but through her responses to my questions. We can truly see that Jesus is around us if we intentionally take time to reflect on the goodness of the Lord. He is the very breath we breathe. That should make us want to shout hallelujah from the top of our lungs.

I have been young, and now am old; yet have I not seen the righteous forsaken, nor his seed begging bread. Psalm 37:25

Everyone should give according to how the Lord God has blessed them. Thank God I learned at a young age that it is more blessed to give than to receive. Mom had so much to give, and she did it extravagantly.

But if anyone does not provide for his own, and especially for those of his household, he has denied the faith and is worse than an unbeliever. 1 Timothy 5:8 NKJV

I have shown you in every way, by laboring like this, that you must support the weak. And

remember the words of the Lord Jesus, that He said, 'It is more blessed to give than to receive.' " Acts: 20:35 NKJV

So many people loved her. Mom lived a life that I can't tell it all. She spent most of her life trying to grow the kingdom of God by ministering to the lost and praying for people to be healed. Through her life, I have learned how to live a holy and righteous life. She was a great ambassador for Christ. She was very obedient, humble, and faithful to God. There was so much expressed through her life that glorified God.

Let your light so shine before men, that they may see your good works and glorify your Father in heaven. Matthew 5:16 NKJV

Blessed are those who hunger and thirst for righteousness, For they shall be filled.
Matthew 5:6 NKJV

But He gives us more grace. This is why it says: "God opposes the proud, but gives grace to the humble." James 4:6 NKJV

Now then, we are ambassadors for Christ, as though God were pleading through us: we implore you on Christ's behalf, be reconciled to God. 2 Corinthian 5:20 NKJV

Oh, have FAITH was one of her favorite statements. Mama was a true woman of FAITH, FAITH, and more FAITH. She told everybody that would listen that you got to have faith and believe God for your healing. Mom truly believed that all things were possible with God and when she prayed, she trusted the Lord would hear her prayers. When we live a life of living by every word that proceeds out of the mouth of God and follow the instructions of Jesus, we can have a prosperous life. Let us be led by the Spirit of God daily, faint not and keep the faith.

What a true honor to have a mother that was so full of faith. Our faith in God can take us places that seem impossible to others, but with God, all things are possible, for He has all power. Oh! Let your faith arise.

So Jesus answered and said to them, "Have faith in God. For assuredly, I say to you, whoever says to this mountain, 'Be removed and be cast into the sea,' and does not doubt in his heart, but believes that those things he says will be done, he will have whatever he says. Therefore I say to you, whatever things you ask when you pray, believe that you receive them, and you will have them. Mark 11:22-24 NKJV

But Jesus looked at them and said to them, "With men this is impossible, but with God all things are possible." Matthew 19:26 NKJV

The righteous cry out, and the Lord hears, And delivers them out of all their troubles.
Psalm 34:17 NKJV

But He answered and said, "It is written, 'Man shall not live by bread alone, but by every word that proceeds from the mouth of God.'"
Matthew 4:4 NKJV

And let us not be weary in well doing: for in due season we shall reap, if we faint not.
Galatians 6:9 NKJV

Oh, what a true jewel that was given to us to show us how God would want His people to follow the example of Jesus. Jesus was very compassionate, and we, too, should live a life full of compassion. It takes a compassionate spirit like Jesus in order to fulfill our purpose here on earth. I'm sure If mom were here today, she would tell us we should show the love Jesus displayed towards us. As well as show compassion as He did toward all mankind. Everybody is somebody in the Lord's eyes. We should continuously make sure we always show sympathy in the time of sorrow and mercy to all who are suffering. That is exactly what God wants us to do.

And there came a leper to him, beseeching him, and kneeling down to him, and saying unto him, If thou wilt, thou canst make me clean. And Jesus, moved with compassion, put forth his hand, and touched him, and saith unto him, I will; be thou clean. And as soon as he had spoken, immediately the leprosy departed from him, and he was cleansed.
Mark 1:40-42

For the poor will never cease from the land; therefore I command you, saying, 'You shall open your hand wide to your brother, to your poor and your needy, in your land.'
Deuteronomy 15:11 NKJV

Harvest upon harvest awaits all of us who carry the heart of Jesus. As Jesus went about teaching, preaching, and healing the sick is a true example of what one can do when they yield to their calling. It may not look like my mom's calling, but it looks like the uniqueness God originally created for you. Jesus said in Matthew that the harvest is plentiful, but the laborers are few. God has given all of us unique gifts that can help bring in a harvest. All we must do is partner with the Holy Spirit and let Him lead us to places we never would have imagined.

† Prayer

Heavenly Father, I come in the name of Jesus, knowing that You are the Lord of the harvest. I am beyond grateful to You for allowing my mom to be a vessel of labor for You. As I have experienced great and abundance harvest before my eyes, I pray that You would pour out Your spirit of compassion and grace upon all with the ability to be laborers for Your harvest. I pray that their desires will be stirred in the direction of the path You created, and they will not turn back but move forward as the Holy Spirit leads. In Jesus' name! Amen.

CHAPTER 4

COLORFUL WALK WITH GOD

Over my lifetime, I have seen many rainbows that amazingly paint the sky with brilliant colors of red, green, white, blue, and gold straight from the hand of God. In awe, I'm always struck with the wonder of ALL His faithful promises that mom always stood upon. I often picture her in great illumination.

One of my fondest memories of mom was her love for red roses. I regularly think of her while working in my rose garden. She was my rose. Roses have a way of stealing your heart away because they are symbolic of love. Oh, how mom just knew the true meaning of how to receive God's love and give it away.

Not only do roses represent love, but they also have a deep red color that just pops with brilliance. Simultaneously, when we study God's word, red often is symbolic of the blood of Jesus, anointing, and healing—perfectly fitting for what mom carried—graced with an anointing full of the blood of Jesus to set His people free. What a powerful God of restoration we have when we stay in a posture of prayer. She exemplified what prayer can do when you make prayer a culture. As Jesus speaks to all of us that men ought to always pray.

Roses also dispense a beautiful aroma, just like mom. Her perfume left a mark. The bible speaks about us spreading God's fragrance everywhere, and it's a true joy knowing that mom made Him evident. Even our prayers should go up with a sweet aroma. I truly believe that mom's prayers reached heaven as a sweet savory aroma.

And he spake a parable unto them to this end, that men ought always to pray, and not to faint. Luke 18:1

Let my prayer be set forth before thee as incense; and the lifting up of my hands as the evening sacrifice. Psalm 141:2

White is one of the many colors that symbolizes worthy of being called purity, holiness, and righteousness. It was a color that mom would wear on special church events, especially on Mother's Day. She would wear white along with the other mothers. I can truly say she was living a life of purity, holiness, and righteousness. She gave so much to all of us. She even prayed into the future of the next generations as well. Holy, holy, holy she was. I am so glad she taught us what a true representation of holiness looked like.

Not only does white represent holiness, but it also represents light. Mom carried the light of Jesus that was not hidden. Jesus even said that He is the light of the world, and He came so that you may have life abundantly. This is so true when I think about all the sick people that came for prayer, and through the light of Jesus, lives were changed. The giver of light showed up and manifested Himself in miraculous ways.

Thou hast a few names even in Sardis which have not defiled their garments; and they shall walk with me in white: for they are worthy. He that overcometh, the same shall be clothed in white raiment; and I will not blot out his name out of the book of life, but I will confess his name before my Father, and before his angels. Revelation 3:4-5

You are the light of the world. A city that is set on a hill cannot be hidden. Matthew 5:14

Then Jesus spoke to them again, saying, "I am the light of the world. He who follows Me shall not walk in darkness, but have the light of life. John 8:12

We as believers should let the light inside shine on the outside so that men may see a reflection of the Lord. Let the light shine in your walk and in your talk that we may become the city Matthew spoke about in Chapter 5. Letting your light overpower the negative things leads to greatness.

Thou hast a few names even in Sardis which have not defiled their garments; and they shall walk with me in white: for they are worthy. He that overcometh, the same shall be clothed in white raiment; and I will not blot out his name out of the book of life, but I will confess his name before my Father, and before his angels.
Revelation 3:4-5

Let your light so shine before men, that they may see your good works, and glorify your Father which is in heaven. Matthew 5:16

Ye are the light of the world. A city that is set on an hill cannot be hid. Matthew 5:14

Gold is another striking color that made mom stand out. In second Timothy, Paul wrote about gold vessels of honor that are fit to be used by God. I praise God for how He blessed me with a mom who chose to be His vessel. The Lord truly blesses us with goodness day by day and puts a crown of gold on our heads. Mom surely wore a gold crown during her lifetime.

But in a great house there are not only vessels of gold and of silver, but also of wood and of earth; and some to honour, and some to dishonour.
2 Timothy 2:20

For You meet him with the blessings of goodness; You set a crown of pure gold upon his head.
Psalm 21:3 NKJV

It is no coincidence that the ark of the covenant was covered in gold. God's pattern for us is to fellowship with Him in proximity is truly a golden treasure. Mom was a true seeker of God's heart. She always found time to draw closer to God. When we take time to draw close to God, He will draw close to us. The healings that took place through her were a result of her consistency in prayer and her strong desire to know God's heart. I can't mention gold without mentioning the color silver. Silver was another shining color within mom's walk. She always believed in ALL God's promises and faithfully stood on them, as mentioned in Psalms twelve. While she endured many tests, God refined her as silver. There was an old gospel hymn called, "Standing On The Promises" that truly resonates in my heart when I think of mom wearing the color silver.

The words of the Lord are pure words: as silver tried in a furnace of earth, purified seven times. Thou shalt keep them, O Lord, thou shalt preserve them from this generation for ever.
Psalm 12:6-7

For You, O God, have tested us; You have refined us as silver is refined. Psalm 66:10 NKJV

Another vivid color that mom walked in was the true mark of blue. Praying for the future of the next generation. Just as the Lord spoke to Moses in Numbers...

> *Speak unto the children of Israel, and bid them that they make them fringes in the borders of their garments throughout their generations, and that they put upon the fringe of the borders a ribband of blue: And it shall be unto you for a fringe, that ye may look upon it, and remember all the commandments of the Lord and do them.* Numbers 15:38-39

It is so important that you and I remember the commandments of God and do exactly as He commands us to do. Our lives have a tremendous impact on generations to come, so let it be a holy life that we live. Mom was sanctified and holy, and the life she lived will live with generations to come. The same manifestation of the Holy Ghost that lived in her is the same Holy Ghost that can live in us and mature us if we so desire Him.

> *Sanctify yourselves therefore, and be ye holy: for I am the Lord your God.* Leviticus 20:7

Mom also loved the color purple, which represents royalty. People saw her as a special woman of God who stood strong in her faith and a believer that had been blessed by God. Peter states that we are a royal priesthood and mom exemplified her priestly role as she spent a lifetime giving praises unto God.

There were many times when I saw mom wearing garments of royalty. A lot of my memories go back to when she would have weekly prayer meetings at our house. We would have wall-to-wall flocks of people in those meetings. We would sing and praise God, and mom would let the Holy

Ghost have His way. She would pray for people to be healed, saved, and for the infilling of the Holy Ghost. God moved powerfully in those days, releasing healing, setting people free, and giving them the Helper. I am so grateful for those days that left a memorial in my heart. How amazing it is to know that the same spirit that raised Jesus from the dead manifested Himself during those days right in my house.

But you are a chosen generation, a royal priesthood, a holy nation, His own special people, that you may proclaim the praises of Him who called you out of darkness into His marvelous light. 1 Peter 2:9 NKJV

She maketh herself coverings of tapestry; her clothing is silk and purple. Proverbs 31:22

But the Comforter, which is the Holy Ghost, whom the Father will send in my name, he shall teach you all things, and bring all things to your remembrance, whatsoever I have said unto you. John 14:26

But if the Spirit of him that raised up Jesus from the dead dwell in you, he that raised up Christ from the dead shall also quicken your mortal bodies by his Spirit that dwelleth in you. Romans 8:11

† Prayer

Heavenly Father, Maker of heaven and earth, I am so grateful for the colorful rainbows that light up the sky that represent Your promises. My heart beats with joy just knowing that You, my Lord, the creator of all things, can paint the most beautiful nature masterpieces for all to enjoy. I am so thankful that You also called each of us Your masterpiece, and today I pray that Your illumination would fill all of us up that we too would light up the world with brilliancy. May we all overflow with colors that reflect who You are. In the name of Jesus.

CHAPTER 5

TRAGEDY CAME

In 1977 tragedy came to our home. It was something that only God could see us through. It was a Sunday evening on August 8, 1977. When mom got home from church, there was a county sheriff's car in the yard. As our family sat in the car, the sheriff came to the car and said, "Mrs. Currie, you are wanted at the Cape Fear Valley Hospital." Now we knew something tragic had happened to my sister, Frances, because she was in the hospital during that time. Everybody began to cry out to the Lord and ask the sheriff what was wrong. Finally, he said, "you need to go to the hospital; something has happened to your daughter, Mary Frances." With tears in her eyes, she said, "what has happened to my daughter?" He proceeded to say, "let's go to the hospital." Mom got in the car, and they headed to the hospital.

Our entire family was pouring tears and hugging one another. We were all feeling like she was dead. Suddenly the yard was filled with extended family members, neighbors, and friends. Everyone was weeping and trying to comfort each other. By this time, everyone knew she was dead and that her husband had killed her. Within the hour, we received the news that her husband had entered the back door of the hospital and shot her. Not just one shot but several shots, taking half of her head off, and when she fell, he continued shooting up and down her body.

Only God could help us through this tragedy. He told us He is our comfort and peace. I have found that to be ever so true. He was and is the only one who could ease the pain. I've learned through the pain just how powerful God is. We have a faithful God who will carry us and always give strength and peace.

Blessed be God, even the Father of our Lord Jesus Christ, the Father of mercies, and the God of all comfort; Who comforteth us in all our tribulation, that we may be able to comfort them which are in any trouble, by the comfort wherewith we ourselves are comforted of God. 2 Corinthians 1:3-4

Peace I leave with you, my peace I give unto you: not as the world giveth, give I unto you. Let not your heart be troubled, neither let it be afraid. John 14:27

The Lord will give strength unto his people; the Lord will bless his people with peace. Psalm 29:11

Mom's heart was full of heaviness; however, she knew the mighty Comforter would carry her through. This had shaken the whole community. Nothing to this extent had ever happened in our community before. The entire community shared the pain we were going through. During these times, there were many tears. Our family really had to stand together as one, pray and trust that God was with us as He promised.

I remember dad crying every day and saying, "he didn't have to murder my child like that." Dad had a hard time dealing with Frances's death. He was a great father. He had five girls and one boy, and he loved all of us so much. He loved mom and often would hide his tears from her. The bible speaks about God keeping our tears in a bottle. There is no doubt in my mind that God remembers all our sorrows because He promised there would be no more death, crying, or pain.

> *Finally, brethren, farewell. Be perfect, be of good comfort, be of one mind, live in peace; and the God of love and peace shall be with you.*
> 2 Corinthians 13:11

> *You number my wanderings; Put my tears into Your bottle; Are they not in Your book?*
> Psalm 56:8 NKJV

> *Blessed are those who mourn, For they shall be comforted.* Matthew 5:4 NKJV

> *And God will wipe away every tear from their eyes; there shall be no more death, nor sorrow, nor crying. There shall be no more pain, for the former things have passed away."*
> Revelation 21:4

Mom became very quiet during those times, and she said that was her way of talking to God in secret. Even the bible states there is a time to be silent, and mom truly exemplified what a relationship with God should look like. Mom was very strong throughout those times. Her faith never weakened. She kept believing that God was her refuge and fortress, and in Him, she put all her trust. As a family, we were not afraid. We all knew that the Lord was always the Almighty Most High in our lives.

There were many sad moments, and even in those times, mom always looked unto the hill which comes with help. We knew it was a praying time for our family, and that's what we did. We would pray Psalm ninety-one each day. This scripture became our foundation, and I pray that you, too, will make it a prayer in your home.

> *He that dwelleth in the secret place of the most High shall abide under the shadow of the*

Almighty. I will say of the Lord, He is my refuge and my fortress: my God; in him will I trust. Surely he shall deliver thee from the snare of the fowler, and from the noisome pestilence. He shall cover thee with his feathers, and under his wings shalt thou trust: his truth shall be thy shield and buckler. Thou shalt not be afraid for the terror by night; nor for the arrow that flieth by day; Nor for the pestilence that walketh in darkness; nor for the destruction that wasteth at noonday. A thousand shall fall at thy side, and ten thousand at thy right hand; but it shall not come nigh thee. Only with thine eyes shalt thou behold and see the reward of the wicked. Because thou hast made the Lord, which is my refuge, even the most high, thy habitation; There shall no evil befall thee, neither shall any plague come nigh thy dwelling. For he shall give his angels charge over thee, to keep thee in all thy ways. They shall bear thee up in their hands, lest thou dash thy foot against a stone. Thou shalt tread upon the lion and adder: the young lion and the dragon shalt thou trample under feet. Because he hath set his love upon me, therefore will I deliver him: I will set him on high, because he hath known my name. He shall call upon me, and I will answer him: I will be with him in trouble; I will deliver him, and honour him. With long life will I satisfy him, and shew him my salvation. Psalm 91

A time to tear, And a time to sew; A time to keep silence, And a time to speak;
Ecclesiastes 3:7 NKJV

It takes a praying woman to stand a test like this. Even through this horrible time, mom resumed praying for sick people. She knew her calling was to continue to be a vessel for the Lord no matter what. Jesus said He would be with you always, even to the end of the world. She truly believed that with all her heart.

As we continued to process this horrible incident, there was so much support from the sheriff's department in both Cumberland and Sampson counties. Their combined effort to ensure our family's safety was outstanding. We had 24-hour surveillance. The whole community and a large host of friends were very supportive during those times. It is written in scripture to weep with those who weep. We all wept together, and this brought more comfort than one could imagine. Even during the funeral services, we had surveillance planes circling the church as well as at our home.

The circumstance was so serious that both sheriff's departments suggested that all family members leave their homes and stay with other family and friends so they could investigate better. We all agreed to the sheriffs' suggestions. We all divided up and stayed with family and friends. This is a true example of God using others to reflect Him as Jehovah Jireh, Our Provider providing shelter in the midst of the storm.

> *Teaching them to observe all things that I have commanded you; and lo, I am with you always, even to the end of the age.*
> Matthew 28:20

> *Rejoice with those who rejoice, and weep with those who weep.* Romans 12:15

Throughout the investigation period, many people called the sheriff's department saying that they had seen her husband's car. That really kept everyone upset, but we kept on praying for the safety of our family. Eventually, they found his car in South Carolina. Inside the car, they found a note that said he was going to kill another family member, me. Now the sheriff wanted to give me more protection. It broke everyone's heart because I had to quit my job. The sheriffs insisted that I would be endangering others, being that I was working around others. As the investigation progressed, the sheriff called a family member to inform us that her husband was a very skilled Army soldier. He explained that he was very skilled at killing, and he would kill anyone who would get in his way. The sheriff also stated that we should plan to come back home, and he guaranteed to heighten protection until we felt safe. Mom insisted that we should continue to have faith and trust that God would protect and take care of all of us. So, we all agreed that it was time to release the sheriff. We gladly told him how grateful we were, but going forward, we were going to trust God to protect us from the enemy. That was a new chapter of life for all of us.

There were still many days that we had to cry out to the Lord for strength. Just like He did for the Israelites, the Lord heard our cries and gave us everything we needed to get through day by day. He is the Light that shines in the darkness. Anytime you feel you are in a dark place, you can trust Him to show up and meet your needs. He never fails. He brought us through the valley and put us on a path of comfort and peace. Anytime fear tried to overshadow us, our God graced us with bravery and strength. Our family grew closer, and we learned how to enjoy our togetherness at a higher level.

The Lord is my light and my salvation; whom shall I fear? the Lord is the strength of my life; of whom shall I be afraid? Psalm 27:1

Fear thou not; for I am with thee: be not dismayed; for I am thy God: I will strengthen thee; yea, I will help thee; yea, I will uphold thee with the right hand of my righteousness. Isaiah 41:10

† Prayer

Heavenly Father, I come in the name of Jesus, knowing that You are the Mighty One who covers us with Your wings. You are the shield that surrounds us with Your protection. Oh Lord, when we are afraid, You are the one in whom we can put our trust. You are our Refuge and Strength. Today I pray for the reader who has forgotten who You are in the midst of the storm. Help them to sense Your presence and know that You are omnipresent, and You come as comfort and peace. Restore them and give them strength to move closer to You and grow into the fullness of who You created them to be. In the name of Jesus.

CHAPTER 6

RECEIVE GOD'S LOVE AND GIVE IT AWAY

Living in a home with a woman of great virtue made it easy to sense God's love and pour it out on others. We had so much nourishing on the love of God there was no way to escape it. Our home was surrounded by a love that only God can grace you with. We always knew God loved us. We recognized that we belonged to Him, and first and foremost, we were His children. We lived with the greatest commandment being exemplified in our life. So revelatory to when one of the Pharisees asked Jesus, "Master, which is the great commandment?" and Jesus responded, "love the Lord with all your heart and with all your soul and with all your mind." This is the kind of love we should all display each day.

Know that the Lord, He is God; It is He who has made us, and not we ourselves; We are His people and the sheep of His pasture.
Psalm 100:3 NKJV

Behold, what manner of love the Father has bestowed on us, that we should be called children of God! Therefore the world does not know us, because it did not know Him.
1John 3:1

Then one of them, a lawyer, asked Him a question, testing Him, and saying, "Teacher, which is the great commandment in the law?"
Jesus said to him, "'You shall love the Lord your God with all your heart, with all your soul, and

with all your mind.' This is the first and great commandment. Matthew 22:35-38 NKJV

Mom taught us the true meaning of God's love. Not only did she and dad love us, but she always told us our heavenly father has unfailing love for us. Pointing way back in Genesis chapter one, we can see that out of God's heart, the entire love creation system was made. Everything God does is good and from His heart of love for us. When we truly know who we are and that we are loved by Him, we can freely receive His love and give it away.

In the beginning, God created the heavens and the earth. The earth was without form and void, and darkness was over the face of the deep. And the Spirit of God was hovering over the face of the waters. And God said, "Let there be light," and there was light. And God saw that the light was good. And God separated the light from the darkness. God called the light Day, and the darkness he called Night. And there was evening and there was morning, the first day. And God said, "Let there be an expanse in the midst of the waters, and let it separate the waters from the waters." And God made the expanse and separated the waters that were under the expanse from the waters that were above the expanse. And it was so. And God called the expanse Heaven. And there was evening and there was morning, the second day. And God said, "Let the waters under the heavens be gathered together into one place, and let the dry land appear." And it was so. God called the dry land Earth, and the waters that were gathered together he called Seas. And God saw that it was good. And God said, "Let the earth sprout vegetation, plants yielding seed, and fruit trees bearing fruit in which is their seed, each according to its kind, on the earth." And it was so. The earth brought forth vegetation, plants yielding seed according to their own kinds, and trees bearing fruit in which is their seed, each according to its kind. And God saw that it was good. And there was evening and there was morning, the third day. And God said, "Let there be lights in the expanse of the heavens to separate the day from the night. And let them be for signs and for seasons, and for days and years, and let them be lights in the expanse of the heavens to give light upon the earth." And it was so. And God made the two great lights—the greater light to rule the day and the lesser light to rule the night—and the stars. And God set them in the expanse of the heavens to give light on the earth, to rule over the day and over the night, and to separate the light from the darkness. And God saw that it was good. And there was evening and there was morning, the fourth day. And God said, "Let the waters swarm with swarms of living creatures, and let birds fly above the earth across the expanse of the heavens." So God created the great sea creatures and every living creature that moves, with which the waters swarm, according to their kinds, and every winged bird according to its kind. And God saw that it was good. And God blessed them, saying, "Be fruitful and multiply and fill the waters in the seas, and let birds multiply on the earth." And there was evening and there was morning, the fifth day. And God said, "Let the earth bring forth living creatures according to their kinds—livestock and creeping things and beasts of the earth according to their kinds." And it was so. And God made the beasts of the earth according to their kinds and the livestock according to their kinds, and everything that creeps on the ground according to its kind. And God saw that it was good. Then God said, "Let us make man in our image, after our likeness. And let them have dominion over the fish of the sea and over the birds of the heavens and over the livestock and over all the earth and over every creeping thing that creeps on the earth." So God created man in his own image, in the image of God he created him; male and female he created them. And God blessed them. And God said to them, "Be fruitful and multiply and fill the earth and subdue it, and have dominion over the fish of the sea and over the birds of the heavens and over every living thing that moves on the earth." And God said, "Behold, I have given you every plant yielding seed that is on the face of all the earth, and every tree with seed in its fruit. You shall have them for food. And to every beast of the earth and to every bird of the heavens and to everything that creeps on the earth, everything that has the breath of life, I have given every green plant for food." And it was so. And God saw everything that he had made, and behold, it was very good. And there was evening and there was morning, the sixth day. Genesis Chapter 1 NKJV

God is our refuge and strength, A very present help in trouble. Psalm 46:1

I will lift up my eyes to the hills. From whence comes my help? My help comes from the Lord, Who made heaven and earth. Psalm 121:1-2

Mom truly loved the Lord with all her heart, and her hungry for Him was undeniable. Her taste buds knew that He was good, and she wanted us to have that same taste. We not only could taste God at home, but we could taste Him at church and feast on His goodness no matter where we went. You don't even have to go anywhere. You can taste God at all times; twenty-four hours a day. It is a true delight just knowing God is omnipresent. If we stop and ponder the opposite of goodness, we can see that it points to satan, that old serpent. Satan is always working in reverse of God's goodness. He is always the opposite, as mom used to say, "wrongsa doubta."

Being around both believers and unbelievers, I discovered that there is a lack of understanding of God's love for us. It's totally heartbreaking to hear some of the same questions being asked over and over in reference to God's love. The question that always seems to be on both sides of the scale; If God is so good and He loves me so much, why did this happen? While, I don't have all the answers to why things happen here on earth, I can say that no matter what, God still loves us the same as He did from the day He created the earth. Nothing will ever separate us from the love of God. Even when our bad choices veer us off the path, His love is everlasting, and His original plan for us remains the same.

Oh, taste and see that the Lord is good; Blessed is the man who trusts in Him!
Psalm 34:8 NKJV

The eyes of the Lord are in every place, Keeping watch on the evil and the good. Proverbs 15:3 NKJV

So the great dragon was cast out, that serpent of old, called the Devil and Satan, who deceives the whole world; he was cast to the earth, and his angels were cast out with him. Revelation 12.9

The Lord hath appeared of old unto me, saying, Yea, I have loved thee with an everlasting love: therefore with lovingkindness have I drawn thee. Jeremiah 31:3

For I am persuaded, that neither death, nor life, nor angels, nor principalities, nor powers, nor things present, nor things to come, Nor height, nor depth, nor any other creature, shall be able to separate us from the love of God, which is in Christ Jesus our Lord. Romans 8:38-39

We still must keep in mind that we were born into a sinful world, but Jesus came and bore our sins as well as diseases that we may live and know the love of the Father. He is the true expression of God. When you look at Jesus you see God. He didn't say we wouldn't have trials and tribulations. Trials and tribulations do not void God's love for us. I think both trials and tribulations prove that through it all, we were made stronger, and our love for God grows even deeper, Simultaneously, giving us opportunities to testify of his everlasting love and grace.

Therefore, just as through one man sin entered the world, and death through sin, and thus death spread to all men, because all sinned. Romans 5:12 NKJV

Who his own self bare our sins in his own body on the tree, that we, being dead to sins, should live unto righteousness: by whose stripes ye were healed. 1 Peter 2:24

Jesus is the greatest example of love that has ever been seen. God is love! Isn't it great to know that God gave us the greatest gift of love? God so loved us that He gave us His only begotten son. Jesus said He is in the Father and the Father is in Him. What a remarkable love connection. We, too, should walk in the same love connection as Jesus. There is so much more for us when we really make God's love connection a reality in our lives. It's God's love that made my mom so compassionate for others. I am driven by God's love to write of His goodness. Oh, how God desires us to know the depth and width of His love endurance.

And we have known and believed the love that God hath to us. God is love; and he that dwelleth in love dwelleth in God, and God in him.
1 John 4:16

I in them, and You in Me; that they may be made perfect in one, and that the world may know that You have sent Me, and have loved them as You have loved Me. John 17:23 NKJV

For God so loved the world, that he gave his only begotten Son, that whosoever believeth in him should not perish, but have everlasting life. John 3:16

May be able to comprehend with all saints what is the breadth, and length, and depth, and height; to know the love of Christ, which passeth

knowledge, that ye might be filled with all the fulness of God. Ephesians 3:18-19

One of the best ways to know God's love is to always keep a picture of Jesus in your heart. When you look at Jesus, you can feel the love of God. Looking from the birth of Jesus and throughout His thirty-three years on earth is the reflection of what God wants us to become. Afterall, we are His children, and Jesus lives in our hearts, crying out Abba Father! Let's take time to STOP, RELAX, REFLECT and RECEIVE love from God daily. This practice will help you make the love connection God so desires from you.

And walk in love, as Christ also hath loved us, and hath given himself for us an offering and a sacrifice to God for a sweetsmelling savour. Ephesians 5:2

And because ye are sons, God hath sent forth the Spirit of his Son into your hearts, crying, Abba, Father. Galatians 4:6

I am crucified with Christ: nevertheless I live; yet not I, but Christ liveth in me: and the life which I now live in the flesh I live by the faith of the Son of God, who loved me, and gave himself for me. Galatians 2:20 NKJV

Behold, what manner of love the Father hath bestowed upon us, that we should be called the sons of God: therefore the world knoweth us not, because it knew him not. Beloved, now are we the sons of God, and it doth not yet appear what we shall be: but we know that, when he shall appear, we shall be like him; for we shall see him as he is. 1 John 3:1-2

As God has filled us with His love capacity, we should truly give it away. Giving love away can be; A simple smile, God bless you, It's a lovely day, How are you today? Can I pray for you? How can I bless you today? just to name a few. Giving love away looks like sweet berries on a vine. Berries that just drip with sweet lustrous juices. In other words, the fruit of the spirit. This is another way to give love away. Let every seed within burst forth the fruit of God's love.

† Prayer

Heavenly Father, I thank You for revealing that our greatest need is love. I am beyond grateful that Your everlasting love is shed aboard and cannot be denied. I know that we belong to You and that You are the greatest Lover of all times. I pray that Jesus may dwell in our hearts by faith and that His love overtakes us and will be forever the fountain that flows like a river that never runs dry. I pray for the one reading this to experience Your river of love that they, too, may gladly receive Your love and give it away just like my mom did during her lifetime. In Jesus' Name!

CHAPTER 7

HOUSE OF PRAYER

As mom continued her ministry journey, she was constantly receiving requests from people in the community about having prayer services. During the late 1970s, several pastors asked her to share a host prayer service at our home. She and another minister started alternating services every other week. This afforded mom the opportunity to have more time for the Lord to manifest Himself outside of church hours. She willingly opened our home to anyone who wanted to attend services on Tuesday nights.

Mom was overjoyed about being a host of the presence of God in our home. She was more than willing to allow the Holy Spirit to have His way. She knew that the Holy Spirit would be the main source of doing what only God could do. She yielded to the new beginnings of a sacred altar at Route 1 Godwin, North Carolina.

Call unto me, and I will answer thee, and show thee great and mighty things, which thou knowest not.
Jeremiah 33:3

However, when He, the Spirit of truth, has come, He will guide you into all truth; for He will not speak on His own authority, but whatever He hears He will speak; and He will tell you things to come.
John 16:13 NKJV

In the Old Testament, you find many of the ancient saints building altars unto the Lord; however, now, as we are New Testament saints, we become an altar, living sacrifices. Our bodies are the temple of the Holy Spirit, we are not our own, and we should always glorify God through it. Mom knew the importance of keeping the fire burning, and during her prayer service days, her desire was to set others aflame. Her vision was that they, too, would be ignited in keeping the flame fresh and flowing through prayer, praise, and worship. As a result, building up a body of Christ that would be sent out to continue growing the kingdom of God.

> *What? know ye not that your body is the temple of the Holy Ghost which is in you, which ye have of God, and ye are not your own? For ye are bought with a price: therefore glorify God in your body, and in your spirit, which are God's.* 1 Corinthians 6:19-20

> *I beseech you therefore, brethren, by the mercies of God, that you present your bodies a living sacrifice, holy, acceptable to God, which is your reasonable service. And do not be conformed to this world, but be transformed by the renewing of your mind, that you may prove what is that good and acceptable and perfect will of God.* Romans 12:1-2

> *But the hour is coming, and now is, when the true worshipers will worship the Father in spirit and truth; for the Father is seeking such to worship Him. God is Spirit, and those who worship Him must worship in spirit and truth."*
> John 4:23-24 NKJV

> *Serve the Lord with gladness; Come before His presence with singing.* Psalm 100:2 NKJV

> *Great is the Lord, and greatly to be praised; And His greatness is unsearchable.*
> *Psalms 145:3 NKJV*

Oh come, let us worship and bow down;
Let us kneel before the Lord our Maker.
Psalm 95:6 NKJV

Mom lived a picture of what Jesus declared in Matthew, "You shall be called a house of prayer." Equivocally, this is also Isaiah's prophecy to Israel. It totally made sense that mom would host prayer services in our home because she was an intentional faithful prayer warrior. Her temple was full of prayer. It was like fire shut up in her bones that would never burn out. I remember seeing her on her knees for long periods of time, sending up prayers to the Lord. Many times, I could hear her lamenting in the middle of the night. While I didn't understand some of the emotions back then, however, I now understand that it was part of her intercessory call. Paul makes it clear about intercessors in first Timothy chapter two verse one "I, exhort therefore, that, first of all, supplications, prayers, intercessions, and giving of thanks, be made for all men." Intercession means that you are standing in the gap for others interceding on their behalf. Mom spent most of her lifetime interceding, and I truly believe that the fruit of her labor is in the midst of us today. She prayed into the future of the next generations.

Rejoicing in hope; patient in tribulation; continuing instant in prayer;
Romans 12:12 NKJV

Therefore, I exhort first of all that supplications, prayers, intercessions, and giving of thanks be made for all men, 1 Timothy 2:1 NKJV

Then I said, "I will not make mention of Him, Nor speak anymore in His name." But His word was in my heart like a burning fire Shut up

in my bones; I was weary of holding it back, And I could not. Jeremiah 20:9 NKJV

During our home Prayer Services, many pastors would come to support mom. People would pack the house from wall to wall. People would show up from the adjacent communities as if it were Sunday morning church services. Collectively, we would have great fellowship together. The bible talks about not forsaking the assemblies and exhorting one another, and this is exactly what our Godwin alter offered. We came together unified in prayer. We sang songs unto the Lord. We lifted His name on high and gave Him lots of praise. God would manifest Himself in powerfully ways. People would be slain in the spirit. Souls would be saved. Some people got filled with the Holy Ghost and spoke in tongues for the first time. I specifically recall one young girl receiving the Holy Ghost, and when she returned home, she was told that it was of the devil. There was a lot of misinterpretation of the Holy Ghost back then and even today.

Prayer is the most important system that we should have in our lives. It is the best way to fellowship with God one on one. We should seek His face and pray without ceasing. A lifestyle of prayer can make a tremendous difference in all situations, even when it looks like there is no way. Scripture says that when we call on the Lord, He will listen. Prayer changes things, and all we must do is ask. Jesus had to pray; therefore, shouldn't we? Jesus tells us that men ought to always pray. It's not a coincidence that the disciples ask Jesus how to pray. Prayer is fellowship with God, and He is delighted when we take time to fellowship with Him.

Then you will call upon Me and go and pray to Me, and I will listen to you. Jeremiah 29:12

Therefore I say to you, whatever things you ask when you pray, believe that you receive them, and you will have them.
Mark 11:24 NKJV

Ask, and it will be given to you; seek, and you will find; knock, and it will be opened to you.
Matthew 7:7 NKJV

Now it came to pass in those days that He went out to the mountain to pray, and continued all night in prayer to God. Luke 6:12 NKJV

Then He spoke a parable to them, that men always ought to pray and not lose heart.
Luke 18:1 NKJV

Seek the Lord and His strength; Seek His face evermore! 1 Chronicles 16:11 NKJV

If My people who are called by My name will humble themselves, and pray and seek My face, and turn from their wicked ways, then I will hear from heaven, and will forgive their sin and heal their land. 2 Chronicles 7:14 NKJV

Rejoice always, pray without ceasing, in everything give thanks; for this is the will of God in Christ Jesus for you.
1 Thessalonians 5:16-18 NKJV

Now this is the confidence that we have in Him, that if we ask anything according to His will, He hears us. And if we know that He hears us, whatever we ask, we know that we have the

petitions that we have asked of Him.
1 John 5:14-15 NKJV

The Lord is near to all who call upon Him, To all who call upon Him in truth.
Psalm 145:18 NKJV

In this manner, therefore, pray: Our Father in heaven, Hallowed be Your name. Your kingdom come. Your will be done on earth as it is in heaven. Give us this day our daily bread. And forgive us our debts, As we forgive our debtors. And do not lead us into temptation, But deliver us from the evil one. For Yours is the kingdom and the power and the glory forever. Amen. Matthew 6: 9-13

It is a true honor that mom opened our home up as an altar for people to come and fellowship. I compared our Godwin altar to the one Abraham built in Chapter 12 of Genesis because there, mom, too, called on the name of the Lord as her source for the prayer services. The Lord showed up and did some miraculous things in our home, and I am forever grateful for what God did back then and what He continues to do today.

† Prayer

Heavenly Father, it is with great honor that I can come to You in prayer. I am beyond grateful for Your faithfulness, mercy, and Your grace that You bestow upon us day by day. Today as I look to You, I pray for all believers and non-believers alike that You would encounter them in a way that they would seek Your face and Your face alone. Help them to know that You are calling on them to come away with You and fellowship. I pray that as they seek You that You would feel them with a strong desire to want the more of what You have to offer them. Help them to know there is nothing in this world that is better than You. I pray as they seek to keep their altar ablaze that they would exemplify the altar pattern Jesus displayed in Your word. I pray this prayer in the name of Jesus.

CHAPTER 8

DESIRING THE HOLY GHOST

I am totally in awe when I think about the well-thought-out plans God created for each one of us. The future He has for all of us is so marvelous. He gave me a remarkable mom, and she continues to impact me day by day. She is not here on earth, but her legacy lives on. She taught me a lot about working with God. The bible talks about how the Lord worked with the disciples confirming His word with signs following. This is also how God's miracle working power flowed through my mom.

We all have a unique ministry, and when we yield to the Holy Spirit, we too can flow in the ministry plans God has for us. Often people think that ministry is within the walls of the church; however, it is so imperative to know that we all have a unique ministry given to us individually. Whether it is in education, business, government, media, and other venues, you can be God's vessel no matter what arena you are in. You can bring in a tremendous harvest as you allow the Holy Spirit to be your guide.

> *And they went out and preached everywhere, the Lord working with them and confirming the word through the accompanying signs.*
> Mark 16:20 NKJV

> *For I know the thoughts that I think toward you, saith the Lord, thoughts for peace, and not of evil, to give you an expected end.* Jeremiah 29:11

Whatever your hand finds to do, do it with your might; for there is no work or device or knowledge or wisdom in the grave where you are going. Ecclesiastes 9:10 NKJV

But you are not in the flesh but in the Spirit, if indeed the Spirit of God dwells in you. Now if anyone does not have the Spirit of Christ, he is not His. Romans 8:9 NKJV

And do not grieve the Holy Spirit of God, by whom you were sealed for the day of redemption. Ephesians 4:30 NKJV

The Holy Spirit is the Lord and is part of the Trinity as written in Genesis One and in the gospel of Matthew. The Trinity consists of the Father, Son, and the Holy Spirit. They all make up the Godhead. Even Paul gives a benediction of what the Godhead looks like for us in Second Corinthians when he says, "The grace of the Lord Jesus Christ, and the love of God, and the communion of the Holy Spirit be with you all." So, when you think of the Holy Spirit, it's important that you see Him as Lord. He is a person, and He has a personality and feelings. The bible says He knows our hearts, thoughts, and secrets. I remember mom telling me not to grieve the Holy Spirit, and now I recognize it was totally scriptural. He has feelings too. It's great knowing that there is nothing that we go through that the Godhead doesn't know about, and God backs up this statement in Psalms twenty-three. This chapter was one of mom's favorite scriptures. It was one of the many chapters we quoted throughout my childhood.

In the beginning God created the heaven and the earth. And the earth was without form, and void;

and darkness was upon the face of the deep. And the Spirit of God moved upon the face of the waters. And God said, Let there be light: and there was light. Genesis 1:1-3

And God said, Let us make man in our image, after our likeness: and let them have dominion over the fish of the sea, and over the fowl of the air, and over the cattle, and over all the earth, and over every creeping thing that creepeth upon the earth. Genesis 1:26

The grace of the Lord Jesus Christ, and the love of God, and the communion of the Holy Spirit be with you all. 2 Corinthians 13:14 NKJV

When He had been baptized, Jesus came up immediately from the water; and behold, the heavens were opened to Him, and He saw the Spirit of God descending like a dove and alighting upon Him And suddenly a voice came from heaven, saying, "This is My beloved Son, in whom I am well pleased." Matthew 3:16-17 NKJV

For what man knoweth the things of a man, save the spirit of man which is in him? even so the things of God knoweth no man, but the Spirit of God. 1 Corinthians 2:11

The Lord is my shepherd; I shall not want. He makes me to lie down in green pastures; He leads me beside then still waters. He restores my soul; He leads me in the paths of righteousness For His name's sake. Yea, though I walk through the valley of the shadow of death

I will fear no evil; For You are with me; Your rod and Your staff, they comfort me. You prepare a table before me in the presence of my enemies; You anoint my head with oil; My cup runs over. Surely goodness and mercy shall follow me All the days of my life; And I will dwell in the house of the Lord Forever. Psalm 23

You will also declare a thing, And it will be established for you; So light will shine on your ways. Job 22:28 NKJV

The grace of the Lord Jesus Christ, and the love of God, and the communion of the Holy Spirit be with you all. 2 Corinthians 13:14 NKJV

    Mom recognized early in her ministry that it was the spirit of the Lord working through her when miraculous miracles were taking place. When the spirit of the Lord is upon you, He can do some marvelous things through you. That is the only way Jesus could do all the miracles, signs, and wonders that are revealed in the bible. When John baptized Him, Jesus immediately came from the water, the heavens opened, and the Spirit of God was upon Him. Thereafter, the Spirit led Him into the wilderness, where He boldly spoke to the devil about what was written. This is a great example of what God's plan is for us. Everything that is written in the word of God is for us, and when we let the Holy Spirit dwell in us, He gives us the confidence to boldly speak what is written. We should make it a habit of speaking God's word over all situations and circumstances. Speaking what is written helps build up our faith and encourages us to endure our race.
    Paul wrote about how profitable scripture is to us in Timothy chapter three. We, too, should hold it close to our heart and agree with everything that is written. When we

allow the Holy Spirit to lead us as we read the word of God, we will be transformed into the image of Christ. That is how we become partners with God. The Holy Spirit partners with God to introduce Jesus to us. He reveals everything that Lord is saying. He will not speak on His own authority but will disclose to you what is to come. Even the Old and New Testament writers were inspired by the Holy Spirit when the bible was written. How else would we have this bible as our guide? Jesus said when the spirit of truth comes, He will guide us in all truth. Holy Spirit reveals all truth to us so that we may become who God originally created us to be. I am so thankful that God didn't leave us hopeless. He gave us this great truth so that we could live a prosperous life.

> *And they went out and preached everywhere, the Lord working with them and confirming the word through the accompanying signs.*
> Mark 16:20 NKJV

> *When He had been baptized, Jesus came up immediately from the water; and behold, the heavens were opened to Him, and He saw the Spirit of God descending like a dove and alighting upon Him And suddenly a voice came from heaven, saying, "This is My beloved Son, in whom I am well pleased."*
> Matthew 3:16-17 NKJV

> *But He answered and said, "It is written, 'Man shall not live by bread alone, but by every word that proceeds from the mouth of God.' "*
> Matthew 4:4 NKJV

> *Thou shalt also decree a thing, and it shall be established unto thee: and the light shall shine upon thy ways.* Job 22:28

Do you not know that those who run in a race all run, but one receives the prize? Run in such a way that you may obtain it. 1 Corinthians 9:24

All Scripture is given by inspiration of God, and is profitable for doctrine, for reproof, for correction, for instruction in righteousness, that the man of God may be complete, thoroughly equipped for every good work. 2 Timothy 3:16-17 NKJV

However, when He, the Spirit of truth, has come, He will guide you into all truth; for He will not speak on His own authority, but whatever He hears He will speak; and He will tell you things to come. John 16:13 NKJV

The more I read scripture, the more it testifies of exactly what mom exemplified when she totally surrendered to the will of the Holy Ghost. When He comes into your life, He is a helper and teacher. In the gospel of John, we see that our father sent us a helper that will teach us ALL things and help us remember what God has spoken. We can all educate ourselves in the word of God; however, it is the scripture and Holy Spirit that produces the living word of God in us and brings revelation. In chapter three of Second Corinthians, we see that the Holy Spirit, also known as the glory of God, is a transformer. Holy Spirit is the one who helps produce in us the fruit of the Spirit, as mentioned in Galatians chapter five. He is responsible for transforming sons and daughters.

But we all, with unveiled face, beholding as in a mirror the glory of the Lord are being transformed into the same image from glory to

glory, just as by the Spirit of the Lord.
2 Corinthians 3:18 NKJV

But the Helper, the Holy Spirit, whom the Father will send in My name, He will teach you all things, and bring to your remembrance all things that I said to you. John 14:26 NKJV

But the fruit of the Spirit is love, joy, peace, longsuffering, kindness, goodness, faithfulness, gentleness, self-control. Against such there is no law. Galatians 5:22-23 NKJV

I witnessed the transformational power of the Holy Ghost in my mom's life, and I'm beyond grateful to have that same transforming power in my life. Growing up, I was serious about my walk with the Lord. In my early twenties, I remember having a strong desire to be filled with the Holy Ghost. So one day, when I was home alone, I knelt down to pray and asked God to give me all that I needed to be a faithful Christian. During my prayer, the Spirit of the Lord fell upon me, and I started speaking in an unknown tongue. Every time I would speak, the words that came out of my mouth were not English at all. The Spirit of the living God started dwelling in me, and it was beyond exhilarating! I could sense the power of God like never before. When mom and dad got home, I didn't mention what had happened; however, that night, as I was praying in my room, my heavenly language began to flow out of me like a river. Dad heard me and ran into the room and knelt beside me, and whispered it's the Holy Ghost. Mom came in and was so overjoyed, and we had a Holy Ghost party right in my bedroom. When we went to church that next Sunday, mom couldn't wait to tell the pastor. He made an announcement, and the whole church gave praises to God.

Ask, and it will be given to you; seek, and you will find; knock, and it will be opened to you. Matthew 7:7 NKJV

Delight yourself also in the Lord, And He shall give you the desires of your heart. Psalm 34:7

For he who speaks in a tongue does not speak to men but to God, for no one understands him; however, in the spirit he speaks mysteries. 1 Corinthians 14:2 NKJV

As I continue to grow in the Holy Spirit, I can truly attest to how the Holy Spirit leads you into your divine destiny. One of my most memorable experiences of how He leads and works through you was when I was asked to go on a mission trip to Africa in 2012. Scripture tells us in Isaiah that you will hear a word behind you giving you direction. I knew if I was going to go to another nation, I needed divine direction. Most importantly is that you always stay connected to the Holy Spirit when making decisions in life. So, I prayed and asked God if I was called to go to Africa. After much prayer, the Holy Spirit gave me permission, and I was released to go, and God said, "I will be with you."

Your ears shall hear a word behind you, saying, "This is the way, walk in it," Whenever you turn to the right hand Or whenever you turn to the left. Isaiah 30:21 NKJV

So do not fear, for I am with you; do not be dismayed, for I am your God. I will strengthen you and help you; I will uphold you with my righteous right hand. Isaiah 41:10 NkjV

From the time my feet hit the ground in Africa, I could sense the Spirit of the Lord upon me. God had truly gone before me and prepared a way for His people to witness His power. Our team was scheduled to minister at the conference for four consecutive days. As the Word was spoken, the Holy Spirit showed up as a deliverer, and many people were set free. The Lord backed up His word as written in second Corinthians; where the Spirit of the Lord is, there is liberty. God worked mightily thought-out all the services. Many people were slain in the Spirit, just like the nights of mom's prayer services. Even the children had a glorious time in the Lord.

Now the Lord is the Spirit; and where the Spirit of the Lord is, there is liberty.
2 Corinthians 3:17

It is a great honor to have been used in another nation as a vessel for the Lord. The Lord truly enriched my spiritual walk during my Africa mission. I often get overjoyed about how the people in Africa totally embraced the Holy Spirit, however, it makes me sad when I think about all the Holy Spirit misconceptions here in the United States. Even during my mom's lifetime, there were many misunderstandings. I think a lot of it stems from wrong teachings as well as the false Holy Spirit behavior extremities. Some of the behaviors that have been paraded in churches have led to disbeliefs, doubts, and fears. Again, those types of mindsets do not come from the Holy Spirit. The Holy Spirit is a gentle gift that reveals the power and presence of God. He makes it possible for an unbeliever to receive Christ. He is the only one who can make God real to us as spoken by the Lord in Zechariah, "not by might nor by power, but by My Spirit." The Holy Spirit makes us who God originally created us to be. What a great and marvelous helper God gifted to All of us. Hallelujah!!!

Another misconception about the Holy Spirt during my mom's lifetime that continues to be misunderstood is the gift of speaking in other tongues. Scripture states that on the day of Pentecost, the apostles were in one place and a sound from heaven as a wind filled the house. They immediately were filled with the Holy Ghost and spoke in other tongues as the Spirit gave them utterance. Some people think that the gift was only for that specific time period; however, in the gospel of Mark, Jesus speaks the Great Commission, which says, "Go into all of the world and preach the gospel to every creature. He who believes and is baptized will be saved; but he who does not believe will be condemned. And these signs will follow those who believe. In my name they shall cast out demons; they should speak with new tongues; they will take up serpents; and if they drink anything deadly, it will by no means hurt them; they will lay hands on the sick, and they will recover." Speaking in tongues is for ALL believers. It is for ALL who has a sincere desire.

When the Day of Pentecost had fully come, they were all with one accord in one place. And suddenly there came a sound from heaven, as of a rushing mighty wind, and it filled the whole house where they were sitting. Then there appeared to them divided tongues, as of fire, and one sat upon each of them. And they were all filled with the Holy Spirit and began to speak with other tongues, as the Spirit gave them utterance. Acts 2:1-4 NKJV

So he answered and said to me: "This is the word of the Lord to Zerubbabel: 'Not by might nor by power, but by My Spirit,' Says the Lord of hosts. Zechariah 4:6

He who believes and is baptized will be saved; but he who does not believe will be condemned. And these signs will follow those who believe: In My name they will cast out demons; they will speak with new tongues; the will take up serpents; and if they drink anything deadly, it will by no means hurt them; they will lay hands on the sick, and they will recover." Mark 16:17-18 NKJV

Speaking in tongues has so many advantages for a believer. It's another one of God's outstanding plans for us to be able to speak directly to Him. Paul states in First Corinthians that "he who speaks in a tongue does not speak to men but to God, for no one understands him; however, in the spirit he speaks mysteries." That is exactly what God's plan is. As we fellowship with the Holy Spirit one on one, He begins to pour out God's individual plan into your spirit. The supernatural language He uses is an unknown tongue spoken out by you. This language helps edify you and ignite you with His power. Paul specifically writes that "he who speaks in a tongue edifies himself and he who prophesies edifies the church." This is how the Holy Spirit helps build us so we become more like Christ. What a remarkable gift God has for ALL believers.

Another advantage of speaking in tongues is to allow the Holy Spirit to pray through us during our private time with God. Paul says, "if I pray in a tongue, my spirit prays, but my understanding is unfruitful." This means that Holy Spirit wants to join us in prayer. This is always the advantage of prayer. That way, we are praying what is on God's heart. Paul also mentions that we can sing with the Spirit. We can stir up the Holy Spirit within us as we worship and send up praises directly to God. These are such refreshing moments in the spirit. Oh, how God has truly given us everything we need and more to live a joyous and peaceful life.

For he who speaks in a tongue does not speak to men but to God, for no one understands him; however, in the spirit he speaks mysteries. 1 Corinthians 14:2 NKJV

He who speaks in a tongue edifies himself, but he who prophesies edifies the church. 1 Corinthians 14:4 NKJV

For if I pray in a tongue, my spirit prays, but my understanding is unfruitful. What is the conclusion then? I will pray with the spirit, and I will also pray with the understanding. I will sing with the spirit, and I will also sing with the understanding. 1 Corinthians 14:14-15 NKJV

Speaking to one another in psalms and hymns and spiritual songs, singing and making melody in your heart to the Lord. Ephesians 5:1

† **Prayer**

Heavenly Father, I am so grateful for Jesus and the Holy Spirit. Oh, how Your great plan is beyond what we can ever repay. I thank You for giving us an opportunity to commune with You through the Holy Spirit. I thank You for the ancient patterns You left for us to get to know Your ways. I thank You for all the faithful ones that have gone before me that exemplified Your goodness. As I look to You this day once again, I am beyond grateful for the Holy Spirit that lives in me. Father, I know You are no respecter of persons as written in Romans. So today, I lift every reader, their families, saved and unsaved people up to You, asking You to stir their desire to want more of You. Help them to know that they can come to You right where they are and cry out to You for more. For You, God of Abraham, Isaac, and Jacob is the same yesterday and today. I ask that the oppressed will be set free and that people all over the world would come to know Your great truth that leads to triumph. In the might name of Jesus.

† Salvation Prayer

For the reader who has read this book and you sense that the Lord is drawing you near know that I am standing in prayer with you. Jesus is also standing with His arms wide open saying come follow me.
    We all were born into sin however, Jesus came and bore our sins on the cross so that we could be reconciled back to our father. As you look to Jesus know that He can save you through faith just like He did for my mom and many others. While, you faithfully stand before Him with a surrender heart you can freely confess with your mouth that Jesus is Lord and truly believe in your heart that God raised Him from the dead you will be saved.
    Sincerely, you can stand before Him and repeat this prayer and make it more personal to fit you....

Lord Jesus, I come before you today with a heart of gratitude thanking you for bearing my sins on the cross. I know I am a sinner and I haven't always walked in alignment to your word but, today I close the door to all things that are not of you . I truly believe that you are the Son of God who died on the cross for my sins and rose from the dead. I am aware that you are alive. Thank you for the gift of eternal life. I open my heart and ask that you come and reside and be my Savior. Amen

CHAPTER 9

POWER OF TESTIMONIES

Many people saw the high level of anointing that mom carried but beyond her calling is the power of testimonies. Testimonies draw people to see the truth that; Jesus is alive, Jesus heals, Jesus saves, Jesus delivers, and Jesus restores. Testifying the goodness of the Lord reveals that the same Jesus that was raised from the dead lives inside of us.

The following is a compiled conglomerate of testimonies that speak of the power of Jesus. In comparison, this is only a portion of testimonies because if I could write them all, there would be never-ending books. I pray that this collection will inspire you to fall deeper in love with Jesus. May your spirit be ignited to testify that others may see that God's power cannot be denied and is here to stay.   Be Blessed...

I was the oldest girl, so I could start when I was growing up. I was a very mischievous child, and I loved to fight. I always wanted my way, but my mother would put me in my place. Back then, we would get whippings. It really did hurt, but she would tell me I needed to obey her. Now I see that she was training me up to be a disciplined person. I love my mother, for she was the greatest mother. She taught me so much; how to live an honest life, work hard, and live a righteous life. I remember my mother praying for me when I had a bad toothache. She would place her fingers in my mouth and pray the prayer of faith, and the pain was gone in minutes. I also remember that there were many people from out of state that would come to our house for prayer. Mother was the greatest mom ever. ~RE

My mother was a good lady. A powerful woman of God with a great anointing. She loved her family. We were the most important thing in her life besides God. She talked to us about the real world but always put God first. She was a good mother, wife, and grandmother. She taught all children about God and doing the right things. She picked me up when I was down, and She took time to pray when I was hurting. She made me smile when I was sad. ~MH

I was the youngest, and I always said, "I'm the baby." My most remembrance about my life growing up with my mother was that she was a woman of God. I thank God for my mother being hard on me and raising me the way she did because now I am living proof that her prayers reached heaven. I remember my aunt telling me how my mother prayed for me all night long because the doctor couldn't do anything to help. Mom's prayers healed me. When the doctors say no, Jesus says YES. This is a good example of when Helen Baylor sang her testimony, "Praying Grandmother," because I had a prayer mother who was also a grandmother.

Mother prayed me through a lot of pain. In my late teens, I was in a horrible motorcycle accident. My knee was badly injured. When I got home from the hospital, I was in horrific pain and could not rest at all. Mother prayed for me, and the pain ceased, and I was able to sleep throughout the night. I am so thankful for a praying mother.

When I got married, I would call my mother about things. She would tell me to pray, and I would say, "I did." Then she would say, "Let God do what He needs to do." I remember lots of good talks with her, and one thing I can say is that she would tell me, "just pray," and she was right. I miss her so much. ~DH

I met my mother-in-law about one year before I married her son. I came to love her. She was a plain spoken person.

After a while, I found out that she prayed for the sick. We started going to different homes. Tuesday night, we went to Sandy Grove, and Wednesday night, we went to Bethlehem. She went any time someone asked her to come to their home. I saw people come in at her home in a great deal of pain. Sometimes it was so bad she would bend her fingers down, and she would sometimes ask me to open her fingers out. She was truly a woman of God. One time I thought I was about three months pregnant and went to the doctor. He said it was gas pockets in my stomach. I went to her house, and I had on a dress with a belt on it. She laid her hands on my stomach and prayed. When I stood up, my belt was down below my stomach. My stomach was back to normal. I have seen many people get healed many times. She prayed for me until she got sick and went home to be with God ~NMC

I grew up in the house with my grandfather and grandmother until I was twelve years old. My grandmother had a unique gift. The gift of laying on of hands and the sick would recover just like the bible said. It was a gift like I've never seen and have never seen again. People would send for her and travel for miles to have her pray for them. She told me once that I traveled with her as a child by train to the state of Virginia so that she could pray for someone. I remember people coming from miles around to our home, and she would pray for them. Let me say why this gift was so unique. When she laid her hand on you, you could feel the pain leaving your body as if she would be drawing it out from you. Sometimes the sickness would even pass from the person through her body and out. I've seen her after praying for someone on her hands and knees throwing up. I've heard her make gastritis sound like belching when sickness passed through her from the person she was praying for. Her hand would draw up and make popping and cracking sounds as if she was cracking her knuckles. I've seen people come to our home, and I've been with her when she has gone to people's homes that were sick. But after she prayed for them, they were healed. It is possible that some of these people could have had diseases that could have killed them. Her gift could have saved their lives. ~LE

As I reflect, when I was a young boy being raised by a grandmother who acknowledged her gift from God, who would turn out to be a vessel for God's miraculous healing power. I witnessed people coming with ailments ranging from common colds to arthritis. I observed her praying for toddlers with pneumonia and would, in turn, throw up their mucus from her own mouth. She never asked for money as special favors, and one of the first things she would say is that "it was not her, it was God, and they had to have faith." I witnessed a lot of miracles as I think back and realize there's no way I can be a non-believer with all I have seen with my own eyes. She lived her purpose and faced the negative as well as the positive from critics and performed God's assignment, and kept her faith throughout it all! ~DGC

I grew up in the house with my granny Clydia Currie. I saw the Lord use her in so many ways so many times! I could never narrow it down to one miracle! Just know that once my grandmother laid her hands on you to pray... God moved! The anointing flowed through her like rivers of running water. I've never seen or known anyone else so pure, humble, and anointed, and I don't think that there ever will be another to fill her shoes. The Lord used her as his temple to heal the sick, give sight to the blind, and I even saw children get up and walk who was told by doctors that they would never walk! Glory to God for blessing me with such an amazing legacy! ~TLD

There have been a lot of well-known God's Generals, such as Smith Wigglesworth, Aimee Semple McPherson, Kathryn

Kuhlman, and Oral Roberts, just to name a few who moved in the power of God during my grandmother's era. I perceived her to one of them in her own right. She didn't have a television ministry or a major spotlight around the world, but God illuminated her in a small town. I'm beyond grateful that God can choose to lift anyone whom others gleam to be plain and simple. My dear grandmother, a black lady from a small town, God used her miraculously to reveal that Jesus is a healer and the Holy Ghost is a maker of man.

The best gift my grandmother gave me was an introduction to Jesus. The very fact that Jesus revealed Himself through her in miracles, signs, and wonders is beyond amazing. Amazingly so, when I think about the times she prayed sickness away in my life. Grandmother was a faithful prayer warrior. There were many nights when I would fall asleep in grandma's bed, and in the middle of the night, I would hear her repeat the name Jesus in a strong bold voice. I knew then grandma was praying through some situations on behalf of others. I'm so grateful to have spent many nights with her. She taught me what the power of prayer could really do. ~CCW

Have Faith in God, Mark 11:22. These are the words I would hear Grandmom say to people when they would come to get prayer for healing some bodily infirmity.

The defining moment as a very young child, not old enough to quite understand what the Word itself meant. I watched a caucasian man come to my grandmom's house with a limp child in his arms. I would always hear my grandmother tell each person that they had to have Faith. Seeing this particular family, looking as if they had lost all hope, all walk out of the door after praying and holding on to those words, have Faith, the limp person walked out of the door full of life with his family. I still could not articulate the fullness of it, but I knew at this point we all needed it. I remember the countless times she prayed for a cousin who *was over the age of two that could not walk. It seemed like overnight, she started walking. I could go on and on, but thankful for the many seeds of Faith and the gift of laying on of hands that God allowed my grandmother to leave with us. During her last night of having her fullness of usage of all her capacity and limbs, she prayed for me and a relative, and we did not know it would be the very last time we would encounter God using her in a miraculous way. I asked for her to Bless me, and she prayed for me but said to me, you are already Blessed. ~VC*

I was a blue baby when I was born. I was born with blue baby syndrome. The doctors gave me a short period of lifetime; however, I am still here to testify of the goodness of the Lord. God's plans for me were greater than my birth medical report. I am so grateful to my praying grandma because she prayed for me through a lot of sickness and health. In my early days, I had seizures and behavioral problems. Thankfully Grandma's faith in God turned these situations into triumphs. I am now forty-eight years old and living my best life yet. ~ LTW

When I would visit my sister, Clydia, it was such a warm atmosphere. I could always go to her house and sleep peacefully. But when I had pain in my body, she would lay hands on me and pray, and the pain would go away.
When my son, Dallas, was 15 months old, he had a fever of 105°, we carried him to Cape fear Valley hospital in Fayetteville, North Carolina. They put ice on him and sent him home. His fever was 103°; we took him to my sister, Clydia's house and spent the night with her. She laid hands on him and prayed for him, and he got better.
If you ever had any kind of pain and went to her, if she laid hands on you, the pain would go away. After our parents passed away, we would go up there on Sunday, and she

would always cook a huge meal. It was always the best, and she made the best chicken feet and rice.
~ CW

I Had a Praying Sister. When I think of my dear sister, Clydia Baggett Currie, one of the memories that stands out in my mind is her gift of laying on of hands for healing. She was an anointed and praying sister that used the gift God gave her to touch and impact the lives of so many, young and old, who came from near and far.

Being in a family with limited access to healthcare, I learned at a very early age about the power of prayer. As a family of eight, that included six children, myself and my husband, Sherman, it seemed as if someone was always sick or had some type of ailment. While I can't possibly count all the times, Clydia prayed for and laid hands on me, my husband, and my children, I would like to share a few examples of God's healing power through his vessel, my praying sister, Clydia.

My oldest son, Herman, was 10 years old, and his face became very swollen and the doctor diagnosed him as having an abscess that was going to require a hospital stay and surgery. During this same time, my husband was also in the hospital, and I was juggling how to care for both of them. My dear and caring sister, Clydia, told me not to worry and that she would go and stay with my son, so I could be with my husband, who was in a different hospital and having surgery. As she sat by my son's bedside, she, of course, used her gift and prayed for him. When I returned to the hospital to check in on my son, I was excited to hear that the doctor had examined him again and determined that surgery was no longer needed! To God Be the Glory!

With the birth of my youngest child, Annette, I had some complications, and my kidneys were shutting down. I remained in the hospital for six weeks, and the doctors didn't think I would survive. Once again, Clydia laid hands on me *and prayed for my healing. That was 56 years ago, and I am still here today!*

My daughter, Faye, had severe asthma that developed later in her adult life. She was having complications with her asthma and had not slept for at least three days. Clydia came by one Sunday afternoon after being led by God to come and pray for Faye. She prayed and laid hands on her, and once she finished, Clydia passed out. Her daughter, Rebecca, told me not to be alarmed and that this had happened before and that Clydia would be fine. She was correct, and once Clydia was alert, she also shared some motherly advice with Faye. Since that day, Faye has never had an asthma attack that severe, and very few asthma flare ups at all.

Years later, when Faye's granddaughter, Makayla, was born and would get severe colds and ear infections, the tradition continued, and off to Clydia's. Faye would go with her granddaughter for prayer.

As I mentioned before, whenever there was sickness in my family, I would gather my children, and we would drive over to Clydia's for prayer. For some reason, several of my children (Herman, Ervin, Sue, and Tracey) would get severe colds and often developed pneumonia. I simply could not afford to take my children to the doctor for every illness, and I believe that Clydia was God's gift to not only my family but our entire community.

There are so many stories to be shared about this strong woman of faith and the lives she touched. In addition to her gift of healing, she was always giving off herself to others. She was a babysitter for my children and grandchildren. She was a nurturer, and being an older sister, she would also provide me with motherly advice.

My family was always welcomed at Clydia's home. My adult children still have fond memories of their many visits and sleepovers that sometimes included chasing chickens, gathering eggs, and participating in the annual Easter egg hunt she held at her home for many years.

I consider it an honor and a privilege to have been blessed with a "Praying Sister" who loved the Lord, was called according to His purpose, and lived out her days being obedient and using her gift for God's Glory. ~BBW

My sister was a very good person. I would go to her house sick and hurting, and while she prayed for me, she would cry and grunt at times, but before I would leave, I would be healed. It was as if she could feel my pain. She would gladly lay hands on anyone who was seeking prayer. Her gift was well-known throughout the neighborhood. I remember how she prayed for me when I was a little boy because I was very sickly. She could discern your pain. I wish she was here now to pray for me. She could cook some of the best food you could ever eat too. I am not much of a talker, but I do know God worked through her hands to heal lots of people. She didn't take any junk either. She would get you straight. ~JRB

We were living up north, and when we traveled south to visit, my son, Christopher, had gotten sick. We didn't know what was wrong with him. He was having bad pains. Mom and dad told us to take him to Aunt Clydia's house, so we took him there. She prayed for him, and while she was praying for him, she kept making a burping noise. Later, she explained to us what the burping noise was while she was praying for him. He had a lot of gas on him. We were really concerned about him, but when we left there, he was better. ~WMS

Aunt Clydia was a woman of God, gifted with the laying on of hands. This is a gift given by God and practiced during times when mostly poor people could not afford to go to doctors. I am not sure just when my aunt received this gift; however, I did witness the healings of others, including infants that she prayed over.

One of the things I admired about my aunt was that when you visited her, you never left without her giving you something to take home with you. Sometimes it was from her garden, and other times it might be from her freezer. She had the gift of giving as well as the gift of healing. She had a positive effect on my life, and I have tried to pattern my life after her in my giving and staying obedient to God's Word.

As I look back on my life from my early childhood up to the present, I can remember the effects of my parent's strong family values and belief in God, which have influenced and shaped my life with spiritual growth and continues to impact my life in so many wonderful and magnificent ways. Attending Divinity School has been and continues to have a profound impact on my life. I am convinced that this is where God wants me to be at this time in my life.

My first conversion happened during a prayer meeting that was being held at my aunt's house. She had received the gift of healing others through the power of the Holy Spirit. Many people with spiritual needs and health problems would visit her, ask for special prayer, and were healed. It was on one of these evenings while she was praying that I encountered my first conversion and was baptized at the age of twelve. I didn't fully understand what happened to me; I had never before experienced the power of the Holy Spirit of "speaking in tongue." My mother and aunt tried to explain to me what had taken place during that prayer meeting, but I didn't fully understand it, even though I had witnessed the miracles God performed through my aunt on many occasions. A change had taken place in my life, but many years would pass before I fully realized that God had placed a special calling on my life with a plan, purpose, and promise that I would be required to fulfill.
~ MM

Remembering a remarkable woman, my aunt, Clydia Baggett Currie. She was a remarkable woman. She was a blessed woman that could cook, sow, and give advice. When she gave advice, it was something to help you. She was a loving person, always with a smile on her face. Most of all, she was graced with the gift of laying on of hands.

I can remember when I was a small child, we lived on a hill on Highway thirteen. Aunt Clydia would always fix a picnic basket, and I would go with her and her entire family to church on the second Sunday of the month in the morning. After church, she would fix the yard up pretty, and we would have a picnic in the yard. Afterwards, we would go to another church.

Most of all, my first memorable experience of her ministry was when I was 12 years old. I remember having pneumonia. My father, her brother, took me to the doctor, and he gave me some medicine. The doctor told daddy to bring me back in a few days if I didn't get better. When I got home, I couldn't eat. I stayed sick and couldn't go to school. In a couple of days, my father took me back to the doctor, and he told him, "she is too weak, and if she didn't eat and gain strength, I don't know if she would make it or not. She has pneumonia." I remember my father bringing me back home and laying me on the couch, and making me comfortable. He told mama that they needed to watch me all night long to see how things go.

During that time, my father was working with tobacco, and he told my mother that day to see if she could help me to eat some soup. The whole day I coughed and spat up stuff. I was so weak that evening, and when dad got home, he told mom to put a dress on me. My mother dressed me, and daddy picked me up in his arms and put me in the car, and took me to Aunt Clydia's house. Daddy took me into her house and asked her to pray for me because the doctor had given up, but he knew with her faith and what God had promised through her, I would be healed. I remember Aunt Clydia telling her oldest girl to put all the children to bed and not to disturb us unless she called. Aunt Clydia laid me on her bed and pulled a chair up beside the bed, and prayed and sought God. As she was praying, it was as if she could feel my pain. Afterwards, she put her hands on my head and pulled back my hair, and asked me how I was feeling? I said, "I'm feeling good, and I'm hungry." She called her oldest daughter to fix me some food, and I was totally healed. I was able to go back to school the next day. Afterwards, I began to think about how Aunt Clydia would Pray for people not only in our family but people would come from all around, even from New York.

I also remember when I was about 16 years old, I was sick again, and daddy took me to her house again. He asked Aunt Clydia to pray for me again. She began to rub me down from my head to the soles of my feet. I remember I was so thirsty, and Aunt Clydia told me to wait while she was praying. She started praying and speaking in a language I didn't understand, and I now realize it is what the Bible called speaking in unknown tongues. She continued to pray, and I could sense something just moving out of my body. I was hungry, and her oldest daughter fixed me a plate of fried chicken, potato salad, and field peas.

When I went to Aunt Clydia's house, I always felt like one of her daughters. She was a true blessing not only to me, the church, the community, but to everybody she would meet. I got home and kept thinking about how weak Aunt Clydia looked after she prayed for me. My daddy explained how the spirit of the Lord worked through her to manifest His healing power.

One time she came to visit me at my house, and she noticed a big fish in the aquarium. She asked me what kind of fish it was, and I said, "a pacu." She asked me where did it come from, and I said, "Out of the ocean, I reckon." She said that the fish is big enough for two people. I will be coming back with my frying pan and some of my grease. I'm going to split that fish and share it will Ella.

I could go on and on about Aunt Clydia, but if you ever meet her, you would love not only for her smile, cooking, sowing, or her advice but most of all for God blessing her to be used to reveal the healing of Jesus. ~DR

My aunt Clydia Currie was a wonderful, amazing woman, healer, and true disciple of God. One of my fondest memories was my wedding day, August 13, 2015.

As I was watching the wedding ceremony through a small window in the door upstairs, I saw my cousin escort my mom to the stage to light the candles.

There was a whisper in my ear from one of the wedding planners that there was someone who was trying to get into the church, but they had already closed the doors, and they would have to stop the wedding to let them in.

I asked who it was, and they said your "Aunt" with uncertainty, "Currie." Joy filled my heart. I immediately, without hesitation, said please let her in. I remember the wedding planner repeating, "you do realize we will need to stop the wedding procession that has already begun." Without hesitation, I told them I was okay with that.

Rewind a little, prior to the wedding procession starting, I was in a different area of the Church, and my sisters had just helped me put my dress on. One of the wedding planners alerted me that it was about to rain, and I needed to go to the car so they could take me around to the entrance where I was supposed to enter.

The clouds did not look too bad to me, but suddenly there were dark clouds, and as soon as I walked into the entrance, it was like the bottom fell out, and it was pouring rain. It did not last long, but it was still very cloudy.

Fast forward: Once my Aunt Clydia entered the Church and took her seat, the wedding procession continued.

As I was about to enter, I remember looking through the glass doors outside and seeing that it was cloudy. Once I got to the top of the stairs for my cousins to walk me down the steps, there was an Angelic light of the sun that beamed from one of the windows at the front of the Church. A feeling came over me, and I knew that was a sign from God and an added blessing from Aunt Clydia.

The next morning as I was carrying my wedding dress to the car, I saw Aunt Clydia in the lobby of the hotel. I went over, and we took a beautiful photo that I will forever cherish. I felt so blessed to have both of my parents and all my brothers and sisters with me on my wedding day. To have Aunt Clydia in attendance was an added blessing. I knew how special it was for her to attend my special day. ~TWJ

Mrs. Clydia was a highly anointed woman of God. She was my friend. She and I shared powerful prayer meetings in our house. She prayed for many people that were healed. She was a good woman of faith. I miss her, but I know she is with the Lord ~IB

I truly miss Mrs. Clydia. I met her when I was having a problem each month or so for some time. I would have very bad pain, but when she prayed for me, I was healed. Every time I was sick, I would go to her for prayer, and I was healed. I told people about her, and many people would go for prayer. I even took my husband and children to her for prayer. We loved her very much. ~SS

A special gift from God. Sister Clydia Currie prayed for many people, including my family. My son, as a baby, was very sick with a very bad cold. I took him to the doctor, and the doctor told me to put him in the hospital if he was not better by Monday. I carried my son on the weekend to see sister Currie. She prayed for him, and when she touched him, the pain would leave him and go to her body. She began to cough up and spit it out. That was a remarkable experience. My son was a lot better when I took him back to the doctor. I shared the story with the doctor; he was so surprised. I *know this was a miracle. Little did she know she was praying for her granddaughter's future husband.* ~EW

Our mother, Williams, was diagnosed with tumors at Cape fear Valley hospital and was scheduled for an operation. In between the scheduled time, she went to Mrs. Clydia to be prayed for and hands laid on her. She went back a week later for the operation, and when the doctor took an x-ray, there were no tumors. She walked out of the hospital totally tumor-free with the help of God and Mrs. Clydia's healing hand. ~ MW family

Remembering my mom and dad and Mrs. Clydia Currie. Mom was a housewife with six children. I recall mom had what I called a seasonal sickness. It was also called asthma. She had many nights when she had trouble breathing. Water poured down her face as her chest jerked up and down. In earlier years, you didn't just jump in the car and go to the hospital every time someone got sick because medical insurance and funds were not available as it is now. Dad was the only one working for our family, so funds were not plentiful. God knew who we were and what we needed. He put healers in the community. One of our very own. She didn't charge a fee; she didn't have you make an appointment, and she didn't have favorites. She was there for all who were in need. Sickness and pain were her specialties. I never knew how she treated mom's sickness; I only knew we went there because mom couldn't breathe calmly. When Mrs. Currie finished visiting with mama, she could breathe calmly, and the jerking in her chest had ceased. What was disturbing was mama was much better, but Mrs. Currie looked weak. I never understood how that could happen. I only hoped it didn't last long. We took mom to see her many times mostly at the beginning of Spring. She was also burdened with asthma after having a child. I remember because I cared for baby after baby for years.

I only wish we still had people who could carry on the work as Mrs. Currie did in earlier years. Gone but not forgotten, Mrs. Currie was a blessing to many people. I'll never forget her and how many times she made mama better from that terrible sickness. It's amazing what God does through his chosen people. I thank God for placing Mrs. Currie in the midst of our midnights of sickness with mom. It was great consolation and relief knowing she was willing to help without hesitation. She was a blessing from God.
~ WM

One Sunday, our senior choir was scheduled to sing at church. I got to the church step and stopped. Sister Clydia came out of nowhere and asked me what was wrong. I told her hemorrhoids. She took me by my hand and prayed a short silent prayer. We walked hand and hand into the church. From that day until now, I haven't had any more problems with hemorrhoids. ~LB

On a Friday night at one o'clock in the morning after smoking crack, I could not relax. My heart was as if it was trying to come out of my neck. I got up and went down to Mrs Clydia's daughter's house and knocked on the door. She let me in and said, "Have you been smoking?" I said, "Yes." She told me that *I wasn't going to make it to the hospital, and she also told me that her mom was there. I went to Mrs. Clydia's bedroom. She was in the bed, but she reached up to put her hand on my neck, and began to pray. Then I said to her it's not doing anything. That's when she told me that I must believe God for deliverance. I started crying out to the Lord, asking Him to put my heart back right like it supposed to be and let my heart beat correctly. I felt like my heart was trying to come out of my neck. I then felt like my heart fell to the bottom of my stomach. I quickly went to the bathroom, and until four o'clock in the morning, I was throwing up. I was completely set free from crack and never had any more since that night.* ~ *RB*

I had battled with sickness throughout growing up. I remember my mama would call sister Clydia for prayer from time to time. This particular time I started having bad headaches, and the headaches would come at 6 pm in the evening. I could go all day, and the headaches will come at 6 pm, and it felt like something was hitting me between my eyes. I had a fever, nausea, and I couldn't eat. I would lay in bed with pain, crying to mama and asking what it is. Mama would pray, and my aunt said we needed to take her to Mrs. Clydia's house.

They took me to the doctor, and the doctor couldn't figure out anything. I have never experienced such a pain in my life. When we went over to Mrs. Clydia's house, it was after 6 pm, and I was having those headaches. She had me sit on the floor with my head on her lap. When she put her hand on my forehead and started praying for me, her fingers started popping. They were just popping. She looked at my mom and said, given the misery that this child is experiencing, I don't know how she is still alive. Her fingers continued popping. I was moaning, and she kept praying and would talk. She told my mom, "this child is chosen; the devil is trying to kill her." The more she talked and prayed, the more the popping in her fingers started slowing down, and after a while, the popping stopped, and I opened my eyes. Usually, when I got like this, the pain would come, and I couldn't see. It was as if someone was nailing a nail between my eyes, but when the popping stopped, the pain stopped. I sat up, and it didn't hurt anymore. Mrs. Clydia said, "The Lord has healed you, the enemy is after you." She told mom that trials and troubles would come in life, but God will deliver me from them. The doctors couldn't understand what had happened, but I can say it was back in 1979, and that hasn't happened anymore.

Another testimony was when my niece, who is about 40-something now, was seven or eight years old and had something wrong with her joints. She started walking like an old woman. She would cry and start running a fever. My sister took her to the doctor and the doctor said she had rheumatoid arthritis. My mom said the devil is a liar. Nikki is also chosen by the Lord. I remember Nikki's fever got so high, about 105. My sister took her over to Mrs. Clydia's house, and she laid hands on Nikki and the fever broke, and her limbs straightened up immediately. She was only seven or eight and walking like an old lady. She was bent over her and humpback. Mrs. Clydia prayed for her, and all the pain left, and Nikki straightened up and was totally healed. She ran track in high school, went to college, got married and had a baby, and is doing well. ~ CAP

CHAPTER 10

PRAYERS

† Prayer *Chapter 1*

Heavenly Father, my creator and my glory, I lift Your name above all things, and I give You praise and honor for being such a good and faithful father. I am so grateful for Jesus and the Holy Spirit that led me to write this book. I lift this book up to You with gratitude for giving me a precious gem that forever shines bright in my heart. I thank You for allowing her to be a vessel for Your kingdom. As I have written this book unto You, I pray that it will be an enlightening inspiration to all readers. May they sense Your presence and grow to know You on a deeper level. I pray that they will forever be blessed beyond measure in the name of Jesus.

† Prayer *Chapter 2*

Heavenly Father, I give You praise and honor for being such a good and faithful father. I am beyond grateful for allowing me to experience the great move of the Holy Ghost in my mom back in the mid-1900s. I thank You for the shepherding minister who mentored my mom with great knowledge and understanding of You as written in Jeremiah 3:15. I thank You for everyone that was healed, every soul that was saved, and everyone who received Your gift of the Holy Ghost. Today I lift everyone who has chosen to read this book. I pray that they, too, will desire to move to a higher level of Your spirit. I pray that You, the Mighty One, would fill everyone who desires to be filled with the Holy Ghost. I pray that You will save every lost soul and increase their hunger for more of You. May You increase Your anointing on all who have already received but have stagnated. In Jesus' Name!

✝ **Prayer** *Chapter 3*

Heavenly Father, I come in the name of Jesus, knowing that You are the Lord of the harvest. I am beyond grateful to You for allowing my mom to be a vessel of labor for You. As I have experienced great and abundance harvest before my eyes, I pray that You would pour out Your spirit of compassion and grace upon all with the ability to be laborers for Your harvest. I pray that their desires will be stirred in the direction of the path You created, and they will not turn back but move forward as the Holy Spirit leads. In Jesus' name! Amen.

✝ **Prayer** *Chapter 4*

Heavenly Father, Maker of heaven and earth, I am so grateful for the colorful rainbows that light up the sky that represent Your promises. My heart beats with joy just knowing that You, my Lord, the creator of all things, can paint the most beautiful nature masterpieces for all to enjoy. I am so thankful that You also called each of us Your masterpiece, and today, I pray that Your illumination would fill all of us up that we, too, would light up the world with brilliance. May we all overflow with colors that reflect who You are. In the name of Jesus.

✝ **Prayer** *Chapter 5*

Heavenly Father, I come in the name of Jesus, knowing that You are the Mighty One who covers us with Your wings. You are the shield that surrounds our protection. Oh Lord, when we are afraid, You are the one in whom we can put our trust. You are our Refuge and Strength. Today I pray for the reader who has forgotten who You are in the midst of the storm. Help them to sense Your presence and know that You are omnipresent, and You have come as comfort and peace. Restore them and give them strength to move closer to You and grow into the fullness of who You created them to be. In the name of Jesus.

† **Prayer** Chapter 6

Heavenly Father, I thank You for revealing that our greatest need is love. I am beyond grateful that Your everlasting love is shed aboard and cannot be denied. I know that we belong to You and that is are the greatest Lover of all times. I pray that Jesus may dwell in their hearts by faith and that His love overtakes them and will be forever the fountain that flows like a river that never runs dry. I pray for the one reading this to experience Your river of love that they, too, may gladly receive Your love and give it away just like my mom did during her lifetime. In Jesus' Name!

† **Prayer** Chapter 7

Heavenly Father, it is with great honor that I can come to You in prayer. I am beyond grateful for Your faithfulness, mercy, and Your grace that You bestow upon us day by day. Today as I look to You, I pray for all believers and non-believers alike that You would encounter them in a way that they would seek Your face and Your face alone. Help them to know that You are calling on them to come away with You and fellowship. I pray that as they seek You that You would feel them with a strong desire to want the more of what You have to offer them. Help them to know there is nothing in this world that is better than You. I pray as they seek to keep their altar ablaze that they would exemplify the altar pattern Jesus displayed in Your word. I pray this prayer in the name of Jesus.

† **Prayer** Chapter 8

Heavenly Father, I am so grateful for Jesus and the Holy Spirit. Oh, how Your great plan is beyond what we can ever repay. I thank You for giving us an opportunity to commune with You through the Holy Spirit. I thank You for the ancient patterns You left for us to get to know Your ways. I thank You for all the faithful ones that have gone before me that exemplified Your goodness. As I look to You this day once again, I am beyond grateful for the Holy Spirit that lives in me. Father, I know You are no respecter of persons as written in Romans. So today, I lift every reader, their families, saved and unsaved people up to You, asking You to stir their desire to want more of You. Help them to know that they can come to You right where they are and cry out to You for more. For You, God of Abraham, Isaac, and Jacob is the same yesterday and today. I ask that the oppressed will be set free and that people all over the world would come to know Your great truth that leads to triumph. In the might name of Jesus.

† **Prayer of Salvation**

For the reader who has read this book and you sense that the Lord is drawing you near know that I am standing in prayer with you. Jesus is also standing with His arms wide open saying come follow me.

We all were born into sin however, Jesus came and bore our sins on the cross so that we could be reconciled back to our father. As you look to Jesus know that He can save you through faith just like He did for my mom and many others. While, you faithfully stand before Him with a surrender heart you can freely confess with your mouth that

Jesus is Lord. If you truly believe in your heart that God raised Him from the dead you will be saved.

Sincerely, you can stand before Him and repeat this prayer and make it more personal to fit you....

Lord Jesus, I come before you today with a heart of gratitude thanking you for bearing my sins on the cross. I know I am a sinner and I haven't always walked in alignment to your word but, today I close the door to all things that are not of you . I truly believe that you are the Son of God who died on the cross for my sins and rose from the dead. I am aware that you are alive. Thank you for the gift of eternal life. I open my heart and ask that you come and reside and be my Savior. Amen

EPILOGUE

Just like rainbows paint beautiful colors in the sky that mesmerize us, mom painted her mark on everyone she met. She went home to be with the Lord on September 6, 2007, but not without leaving a celebration mark on our hearts. She left a mark that I will forever cherish. Her funeral service was by far one of the most anointed services I have ever witnessed. The Holy Spirit fell upon us, and it was like if we had asked anything of the Lord at that moment, we would have received it. After the service, many said they had never witnessed a homegoing service like that before. One person said that there was a cloud that covered the church. Once again, it was a great move of the glory of God. As the church praised God, it was as if the window of heaven had opened to receive mom. She will never be forgotten, and her legacy lives on.

To those who still have a mother here on earth, cherish the time you have together. Losing a mother is hard when you can't talk to her anymore, but with the Lord, you can make it. If it had not been for the Lord that kept me, I could not have made it. I remember mom told me with tears in her eyes it's not the same when your father and mother are gone. Now, I witness that pain. As you continue to cherish your mom, spread everlasting love on her, and make endless happy memories. Those memories will help you endure when you can't see her anymore.

THE ANOINTED ONE OF MANY COLORS

She is more Precious than rubies: Nothing you desire can Compare with her.
Proverbs 3:15

THE ANOINTED ONE OF MANY COLORS

THE ANOINTED ONE OF MANY COLORS

THE ANOINTED ONE OF MANY COLORS

THE ANOINTED ONE OF MANY COLORS

THE ANOINTED ONE OF MANY COLORS

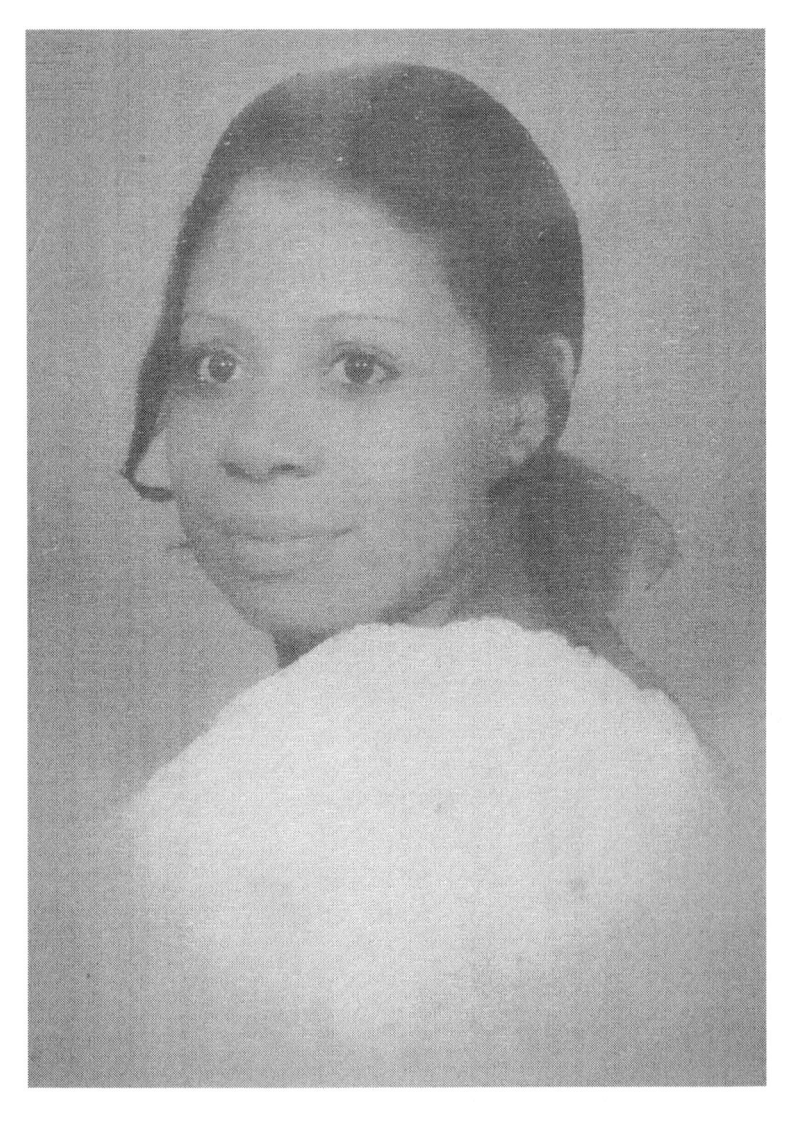

Mary Frances Lantigua March 21, 1952 - August 7, 1977
"Gone But Not Forgotten"

THE ANOINTED ONE OF MANY COLORS

Smokehouse Built in 1969, "Jehovah Jireh"

ABOUT THE AUTHOR

Minister Johnson grew up in a faithful home. Her parents were devoted members of Sandy Grove Free Will Baptist church in Wade, North Carolina. Her mother was known for her gift of faith, and many were healed through her ministry. Under that influence, Minister Johnson surrendered her life to Christ at the age of twelve and was baptized shortly afterwards.

Ella Currie-Johnson graduated from World Harvest Bible College in Columbus, Ohio. Minister Johnson, also known as "Mother Grace," is a spiritual mother to the motherless. Her heart continues to beat with Father God as she journeys with individuals through some of the darkest moments in their lives. She is a mighty woman of valor and is used as a conduit of God's Glory. She is a faithful volunteer in the Cumberland County jail system, where she teaches the Gospel of our Lord Jesus. Minister Johnson has also been involved in missionary work under the Future life Christian Ministries located in Siaya, Kenya, East Africa. There she ministered in a 10-day Women's Conference where many chains were broken, and multitudes were set free.

Minister Johnson believes in the Power of God's Word and Anointing. She has been a true vessel of healing, deliverance, and full restoration of mind, body, and soul. Minister Johnson, having faced some of life's most challenging detours and some tragedy in her race, is a true testament to God's faithfulness. Her story is that of a surrendered woman of God who, through the help of her Counselor, Jesus, raised three God Fearing children as a single parent. She understands sacrifice, faith, resisting temptation, and holy living. Minister Johnson has been raised up for such a time as this to proclaim the gospel and set captives free. She displays a true message that enduring the Good Fight of Faith proves God is faithful and true for all those who believe.

www.ellacurriejohnson.com

Made in the USA
Columbia, SC
13 January 2025